ENLIGHTENED

Dressage as Mental, Physical, Emotional, and Spiritual Development for Horse and Rider

by
Barbi Breen-Gurley
and
Janet Emmons, M.S.

Illustrated by
Paula Zima

ENLIGHTENED RIDING

First Edition
Printed and bound in the United States of America

Barbi Breen-Gurley
P.O. Box 6021, Los Osos, CA 93412
www.SeaHorseRanch.com

Janet Emmons, M.S.

ISBN 0-9742345-0-8

Photography:	David Ball	Tom Meinhold
	Paula Chmura	Terry Miller
	Chuck Jennings	David Nelson
	Robina Mapstone	Sheri Scott

Cover & Book design, and Production and prepress: Pandora & Company, Los Osos, CA
www.PandoraAndCompany.com

Printing: Thomson-Shore, Inc., Dexter, MI
www.tshore.com

Foreword

Dr. Reiner Klimke promised to write a foreword to our book *Enlightened Riding*, when Barbi visited him in the summer of 1999. Soon after her return home from Germany, she heard of Dr. Klimke's death. Shortly after the sad news, Barbi received a letter from Dr. Klimke's son, Rolf. He spoke of his father's strong desire to complete his promised task. Apparently Dr. Klimke managed to write a short foreword while hospitalized from a heart attack. Unfortunately a second attack, a few days later, took his life.

Left to right:
Linda Tellington-Jones, Barbi Breen-Gurley on Majic, and Dr. Reiner Klimke

"*Speaking as a rider, teacher and trainer, I was delighted to read* Enlightened Riding. *Much has been written about the technical execution of movements. Barbi's book offers us a broader perspective. It expands the reader's awareness of the unseen, inner aspects of the rider's thoughts and feelings, which impact both the horse and the rider. The many stories and quotes throughout the book provided by Barbi's students, as well as her own personal experiences, show that Barbi both teaches and lives this approach to riding. The many insights and practical tools presented here are useful not only in our riding, but in life as well. I recommend this book for any riders who want to create greater pleasure and harmony for themselves and their horses, both in riding and living.*"

— Reiner Klimke,
many time Olympic Gold Medallist and author.

Dedication

This book is dedicated to Barbi's father Milton George Apel, who promised a little 4-year-old girl that when she turned 13, she would have her very own horse. Because he kept his word, Barbi has had a joyfully enriched life centered around horses. Her hope is that some of her experiences and lessons can be passed forward offering some insight to other horse enthusiasts, as they grow together with their equine partners.

Thanks

I want to sincerely thank all those who helped me bring this book to completion. Foremost, and with a triumphant sigh of relief from a long journey, I wish to thank my co-author, Jan. She encouraged the idea of "a holistic approach" to dressage several years ago. The long hours working together were much easier working as a team.

Thanks to all my students and instructors, who through the years enriched me in clarity. Initially my path was lit through fourteen years of diligently working with Hilda Gurney. I learned and cemented a foundation of correct basics and the spirit to creatively improve what I have at the moment with myself and my horse.

Thanks to Paula Zima, our illustrator, whose drawings and cover artwork add such a delightful charm to the book. Her background as a dressage rider helped her translate our ideas into apt images.

Many thanks to Pandora Nash-Karner and Cynthia Milhem of Pandora & Company for a fine job with the graphic design and typesetting.

Thanks as well to the several photographers – Chuck Jennings, Robina Mapstone, Tom Meinhold, Sheri Scott, Paula Chmura, Terry Miller, David Nelson, and David Ball – who have contributed such fine images to clarify each example.

Thanks to my mother Tola Apel for her belief that I could complete the book. And, thanks to my daughters Suraya and Chelsea, who posed for hours demonstrating the stretching exercises that we've learned in our years of dancing.

And, last but certainly not least, I gratefully thank my best friend and endlessly giving husband, Geof, for his enormous support in completing this book. Never discouraged, too tired, or too busy, as always, he came through in helping our book become a reality.

— Barbi Breen-Gurley

Preface

Enlightened Riding, Dressage as Development for Horse and Rider presents a comprehensive view of dressage, exploring the physical, mental, emotional and spiritual benefits of dressage for horse and rider. As a licensed S Dressage judge, FEI rider, trainer, instructor, and owner of Sea Horse Ranch, Barbi brings an in-depth knowledge of the physical and mental aspects of dressage to this book. Janet, a Marriage and Family Counselor, who specializes in sports psychology, extends the scope of the book to include a deeper understanding of the emotional and spiritual aspects of dressage. Although many of these ideas are timeless, their vision is unique. They explore the inter-play between the physical, mental, emotional and spiritual dimensions of riding and give practical methods for overcoming blocks along the road of riding development. They also evoke the sense of harmony and beauty that provides the philosophical context for this journey.

Since this approach stems from their experiences and those of many of Barbi's riding students and Janet's clients, the abstract principles of dressage become concrete through many personal stories. Some names are fictitious, but the examples are true. Throughout the book, readers will hear about the challenges many of the students at Sea Horse Ranch face. A delightful humility, a sense of humor, a commitment to grow and a desire to experience the lightness and harmony of riding characterize these riders.

Barbi brings a wealth of knowledge and experience as a trainer and competitive rider. Since obtaining her BHSAI from Moat House, England in 1970, she has taught dressage to students of all ages, abilities and riding goals. Many internationally known instructors such as Hilda Gurney, Robert Dover, Laurie Doyle, and Albrecht Heidemann, have helped Barbi develop her riding skills. Barbi has trained several horses to the Grand-Prix level and won numerous, state, regional and national championships. She is a USDF Bronze, Silver & Gold Medallist. She has twice been long listed with the US Equestrian Team and has been on the Developing Rider List four times.

Janet Emmons obtained her M.A. in English and Educational Specialist degree from the University of Iowa. She completed her M.S. in Psychology from California Polytechnic University. In her private practice, she has worked with many equestrians, helping them overcome fear, performance anxiety, low self-esteem, anger and other emotional blocks to their riding progress. She has trained with Barbi since 1986. Her own experiences as a therapist and rider helped her realize that dressage is a great metaphor of life. The challenges we face in riding, such as staying centered, improving our connection, and preparing for transitions have implications for the way we conduct our lives.

Paula Zima states that her mission is "to create delightful art for the world to enjoy." She has done this through her illustrations, public art, sculpture, and paintings. She has been a dressage and horsemanship enthusiast for many years, and credits Barbi for teaching her a firm foundation in the art of dressage.

— Pandora Nash-Karner,
Editor

“This remarkable book will make you a better rider!”

— Camille Mongeau, student

“Bravo, finally a true masterpiece of interplay and intricate insights from a rider and trainer (not an arm chair quarterback), into a rider's spirit, problems and motivation and the horse's innermost being. A triumph in the explanation of the dance partnership of spirit-to-spirit and heart-to-heart of horse and rider.”

***Gail Alterwitz**, student*

“In *Enlightened Riding*, Barbi Breen-Gurley informs and educates through a classical approach, providing the tools necessary to rise to any challenge. The book illustrates how dressage embodies not just the physical, but mental, emotional, and spiritual being as well. It mirrors the thin veneer that lies between lessons and rewards of dressage and those of life itself.”

***Sharon Kroll**, student*

“As a beginning rider, I find *Enlightened Riding* both instructional and inspiring. It's clear explanation of the art and practice of dressage helps demystify the nuances of communication between horse and rider. Its engaging discussions on the holistic aspects of riding can motivate riders of all levels in a better understanding of themselves and other aspects of their lives. This book is an absolute read for any rider and horse enthusiast.”

***Hedi Parafina**, student*

“I feel extremely fortunate to have been a student of Barbi's for the last twelve years. She has the gift of not only being a beautiful and talented rider, but also possesses the ability to effectively instruct her students. Through her teaching, we learn about harmony with our partners as well as the importance of good foundation skills. This book is an extension of her abilities and will enable many more dressage enthusiasts to share in Barbi's knowledge.”

***Bonnie Krueger**, student*

“I have read many books that dealt with the mechanics of dressage in a knowledgeable and comprehensive way. However, this is the first book that successfully integrates and elucidates the physical, psychological, and spiritual aspects of the journey that anyone who aspires to mastery in the art of dressage must undergo.”

***Susan Travis**, student*

“I found *Enlightened Riding* to have a gentle, humorous vein throughout. The authors' choice of what and how to illustrate various ideas was excellent. The book will be a great addition to the existing body of literature that addresses dressage and horsemanship.”

***Paula Zima**, student*

“I have been working with Barbi for some time and have found that her knowledge and insight into the horse-rider team has proven to develop very positive results. She has the ability to know and explain WHAT is needed to progress and what to have the rider do, HOW the rider must perform for the horse to respond correctly, and WHY the action works to get the desired results.”

***Eldon Kordes**, student*

Table of Contents

Chapter 1 Introducing Enlightened Riding 1

Chapter 2 Why Dressage? 3

Dressage as Relationship 4

Chapter 3 Dressage As Holistic Development 9

Mental Development 9

Physical Development 11

Emotional Development 17

Spiritual Development 22

Chapter 4 Selecting A Trainer 25

Chapter 5 What is: Assessment of Rider And Horse 29

Ancient Wisdom 29

Past and Future Inform the Present 30

Assessment of Rider 33–34

Assessment of Horse 34–35

Red Flag Variables 35

Highly Influential Basic Variables 36

Self Assessment 37

Assessment Conclusions 38

Chapter 6 The Rider's Position 39

Mirror Mirror on the Wall: Assessment of Body Basics 39

Chapter 7 Stretch Toward Supple Riding, Floor Exercises 47

Stretching Safely 48

Neutral Position 48

Neck Stretches 48–50

Shoulders 50–53

Ribs and Waist Isolations 54–55

Hip Stretches 56–58
Lateral Side Stretches 59–60
Leg Stretches 61–64

Chapter 8 Lungeing The Horse 65
Observing Your Horse's Progress 68

Chapter 9 Lungeing The Rider: Mounted Exercises 71
Upper Body Stretches 73–74
Leg Exercises 74–75
Developing the Seat 75
Developing the Effect of the Seat 76
Transitions Within the Gaits 77

Chapter 10 The Aids 79

Chapter 11 Understanding and Improving The Gaits 85
Developing the Walk 86
Developing the Trot 88
Developing the Canter 92

Chapter 12 The Wisdom Behind Winning 95
Physical Preparation 95
Mental Preparation 96
Emotional Preparation 97
Spiritual Preparation 102

Chapter 13 Reflections on Life Lessons 105

Glossary of Terms 113

References 119

About the Authors 128

About the Illustrator 128

1 Introducing Enlightened Riding

> "*More than any other art, classic riding is connected to the wisdom of living because so many of its principles are maxims for living as well.*
>
> *– Dr. Josef Knipp*"

Welcome to Sea Horse Ranch. Overlooking Morro Bay, the dressage arena is a clearly defined space, surrounded by the expanse of hills covered with chaparral and the endless blue horizon of the Pacific Ocean. Nature's presence reminds the riders that nothing is constant: the fog, the tides and the shifting sand speak of continual change. Through change, we are challenged to grow; physically, mentally, emotionally and spiritually. What better place for the conception of a holistic approach to riding! *Enlightened Riding* combines the basics of dressage, which emphasizes physical and mental skills, and the lessons of emotional growth and spiritual practice. This is particularly important not only to beginning riders, but also for those who seriously want to improve their skills and effectiveness.

Barbi's and Janet's holistic approach to dressage emerged over more than a decade of exploring emotional and spiritual issues while riding together. Serving as each other's teachers, Barbi helped Janet, a beginning rider, develop her knowledge and skills in dressage. Janet shared her insights, gained through the study of psychology and spiritual traditions, about dressage's ability to stimulate emotional and spiritual growth. Barbi, Janet and the other riders at Sea Horse Ranch experience valuable life lessons while they progress through the levels. As you explore the chapters of *Enlightened Riding*, you'll encounter a collage of valuable insights learned from two of our greatest instructors; dressage and life. As one of our favorite riding T shirts declares, "Life is a test. Dressage riders take life one test at a time."

Living and working at Sea Horse Ranch since 1971, Barbi has developed her own equestrian skills, trained a variety of horses to Grand Prix, and taught many students of all ages and abilities. The students boarding at Sea Horse Ranch are usually beginning to intermediate riders. Their horses are often backyard pets, untrained or problem horses. Unable to afford an upper end performance horse, they learn dressage on what they have. Teaching riders the basics of dressage is the most predictable part of the journey. Predicting the outcome of what some of these horses can produce is much more of an unknown. Attributes such as patience, commitment, discipline, creativity, self-introspection, fairness, and hard work produce impressive growth for both horses and riders.

Trainers learn as much from their students (horses and riders) as students learn from their trainers. This is also true of therapists. As therapists accompany their clients on an emotional and spiritual journey, they grow in their understanding of this process. Janet's many equestrian clients have illuminated the role of emotional or spiritual blocks, which prevent effective living and riding. We're grateful to the many students and clients who have contributed to *Enlightened Riding*, offering to share their experiences for the benefit of other riders. Perhaps you will see yourself reflected in one or more of their stories.

In the following pages, we hope you'll join us as we learn and grow physically, mentally, emotionally and spiritually at Sea Horse Ranch. We cover all these areas, skimming the surface in order to gain a glimpse of the depth of growth offered by approaching riding holistically. Our hope is that you will gain a deeper appreciation of how the pursuit of dressage can contribute to your personal development and benefit your equestrian partner.

Barbi and Janet performing a Pas de Deux.

2

Why Dressage?

> *It is moving within a multitude of sensations and forces effortlessly, fluidly, without a trace of inappropriate exertion or tension. It is being danced by God at each moment, pirouetting, leaping, eluding all forces that work to trip up and snare the Dancer.*
>
> *–Robin Carlsen*

Whether you're considering learning dressage or aspiring to perfect a pirouette, perhaps you have a picture in mind that inspires you. Janet recalls the moment of her inspiration; watching Barbi and Celebrate perform a musical freestyle to Vivaldi's Four Seasons. "When I first met Barbi, I had more love of horses than experience as a rider. As Barbi rode, she seemed transformed into a Centaur and without the slightest visible effort, directed all four of Celebrate's legs as if they were her own. Together they performed intricate, graceful movements as one: A sense of harmony, joy, and love emanated from them. *(Photo 1)* I was transfixed! I too wanted to become part of something larger than myself, to transcend my limitations and share this fusion of energy with the horse, that magical, mystical creature that I have always loved."

What exactly is it that produces such a harmonious image? At first, dressage is a mystery. The aids seem invisible and the uninitiated observer is at a loss to determine why the horse moves the way he does. Often dressage is defined by referring to the French word Dresseur, meaning training. Yes, it is a systematic method of training a horse, but this definition alone, fails to convey the essence of dressage.

The answer to our question can be illustrated by comparing dressage to a pyramid. The Egyptians first discovered geometric symmetry basic to nature. The pyramid numerically symbolizes the harmony of nature. The symmetrical form of the pyramids have inspired humankind for centuries. The pyramid, conveying symmetry and harmony, points to the essence of dressage. We can extend this comparison to help us understand the separate components of dressage. A pyramid is constructed of four walls, each having two sides. The inner and outer sides of each

Photo 1 — *Barbi and Celebrate in unity.*

wall stand for the horse and rider. Although the inner and outer surfaces are distinct and appear separate, in reality, they're connected.

The connection or relationship between horse and rider is paramount in dressage. The four sides of the pyramid represent four aspects of being; mental, physical, emotional and spiritual. Both horse and rider develop their mental, physical, emotional and spiritual qualities through dressage training. *(Illustration A)* Finally, a pyramid is characterized by tiers of stone, each tier ascending like stair steps to the apex. These tiers correspond to the nine progressive levels of dressage from Training Level to Grand Prix. Training level forms the broad base, with successive levels adding onto this base. Each of these levels, requires a finer tuning of all four of these aspects of being. The Grand Prix performance, or apex of the pyramid, illustrates mental focus and presence, emotional calmness and vitality, and physical balance, agility, strength and suppleness. When these three aspects fuse in the moment of performance, a spiritual oneness may be experienced. At this level the physical, emotional, mental, and spiritual aspects of both horse and rider meet at one point, transforming them into a harmonious expression of unity. This is the ultimate achievement of dressage. *(Illustration B)*

Dressage as Relationship

"Love alone is capable of uniting living beings in such a way as to complete and fulfill them, for it alone takes them and joins them by what is deepest in themselves."

–Pierre Teilhard De Chardin

The relationship of horse and rider is essential to dressage. In riding, two different species join in mutual understanding, physical connection, and enthusiasm to perform intricate movements. The relationship between the horse and rider, as well as the individual development of both, promotes progress to the higher levels of dressage. This relationship forms the connection between the inner or human side and the outer or equine side of the pyramid's four walls.

In *Accepting Each Other*, Michael L. Emmons, Ph.D. and Robert E. Alberti, Ph.D., explain the ACCEPT foundation of a loving relationship between two people. ACCEPT is an acronym for

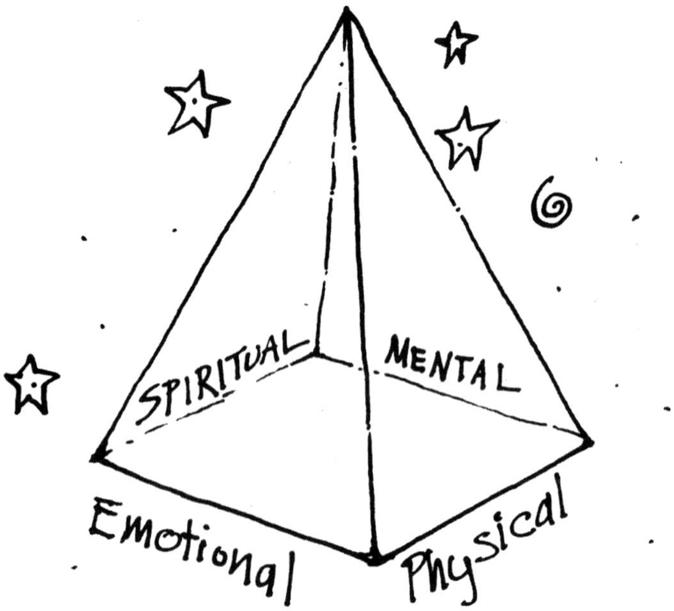

Illustration A. A *pyramid illustrates the 4 aspects of being.*

Illustration B. *The tiers of the pyramid represent the levels of dressage.*

Illustration C. *The accept model of relationships.*

Attraction, Communication, Commitment, Enjoyment, Purpose, and Trust. In the ACCEPT model, these are the concepts for the basis for a loving relationship. As equestrians, we can learn from this model. *(Illustration C)*

Attraction initiates and maintains relationships. Most of us have had the experience of "falling in love" with a special horse. It's often hard to define that attraction. Perhaps its the horse's physical appearance: his size, color, breed, or conformation. Then again, it might be his personality; the spark of excitement or the deep reflection of trust in his eyes, his sense of humor when he tosses your hat in the air, or his easy going, reliable calm. You may or may not have chosen your mount with dressage in mind. That's okay! Although some horses naturally find dressage easier, most horses can benefit from dressage. Do what you can, with what you have, where you are. During your dressage training, continually remind yourself of your horse's attractive qualities. Build a positive mind-set that enhances the relationship. *(Photo 2)* Bonded from Ballerina's birth, Suraya and Ballerina share a loving connection.

Communication allows two parties in a relationship to convey their perspective and understand the opposite perspective. When communication is clear, direct, and responsible, the relationship grows. Dressage offers a language of communication. The rider must first learn this system of communication and then translate this learning into physical action, which teaches this system to the horse. In order to do this, the rider must work through any cognitive, emotional, or physical blocks that prevent this from happening. If the rider has difficulty in any of the four areas (mental, emotional, physical or spiritual) communication breaks down and progress halts. The horse also may fail to respond to communication due to his own blocks. Since the rider initiates and directs the relationship, it is the rider's responsibility to deal with any communication difficulties, whether they originate from the horse or the rider. This begins with looking at our part in either the success or failure of the training program. If we are ignorant of the proper aids, physically imbalanced, impatient, or unobservant, we certainty can't expect the horse to take care of us.

Commitment measures how much you value the relationship and the amount of effort you are willing to give it. Dressage constantly tests the

Photo 2 — *Suraya and Ballerina share a mutual attraction.*

rider's commitment. Achieving focus, calmness, agility, strength, suppleness and lightness require a high level of commitment. Some days we will feel less motivated. Perhaps we have other priorities and it would be easier to leave Equus in the pasture. Maybe two weeks of rain make it inconvenient to trudge around in the slush. (*Photo 3)* All of us balance a variety of demands that take their toll on commitment. Barbi recalls driving her vehicle into the arena, and filling it with toys for her preschoolers. She would then ride circles around the car, keeping an eye on the children while they played. Not only was this a game for her children, she realized many aspects of the Grand Prix could be ridden in a circle. Our level of commitment inevitably affects the relationship. After two weeks off, our horse may be stiff or hot. That's okay, as long as we acknowledge our part in our horse's noncompliance. Remember that it wasn't his idea to pace the paddock the last two weeks.

Photo 3 — *Schooling in the Rain.*

Photo 4 — *Dressage enhances the enjoyment of riding.*

Enjoyment is essential for both the horse and rider. Dressage definitely enhances the enjoyment of riding. (*Photo 4)* When we become balanced and sensitive riders, our pleasure increases, as does the pleasure of our horse. Although dressage sets up successive goals, it would be a mistake to focus exclusively on these goals instead of the process. Dressage offers a forum for the serious competitive rider on the local, national and international scene. However, choosing this as a goal involves a high degree of cost in the areas of finance, focus, and family support. When this goal becomes exclusive, the balance between process and goal may become imbalanced. The true spirit of dressage stresses more how we ride than what level of movement we ride. When we become too goal focused, we may forget to enjoy the process. However, life is made up largely of process. The paradoxical Chinese curse of "May you achieve all your goals," emphasizes that once all goals are attained, the adventure ends. Remember that getting there provides the daily enjoyment of riding.

We must also consider enjoyment from the horse's point of view. Learning suppleness, discipline, balance, engagement, and collection can be difficult for any horse, especially for one that is stiff, uneducated or previously improperly trained. There may be times, through the training process, when the horse may experience difficulty or confusion. The result may cause temporary disharmony or resistance. The rider must be competent, effective, patient, and wise in assisting the horse through these difficult times. Many sources such as accurate instruction from a more experienced coach, videos, and books help create solutions. Variety of lessons also helps alleviate the intensity and focus that schooling requires. We can vary the location and context of training sessions, as well as the activity. Trail riding, lunging, group riding, and jumping offer alternative focus for horse and rider. *(Photo 5)*

Purpose provides powerful motivation. Purpose gives us focus and helps us set goals. We need to assess whether or not our horse shares our purpose. If we have competitive aspirations and want to show at second level, does our horse seem suited to this work? We need to be honest with ourselves. Although most horses can benefit from dressage, not all horses will show an enthusiasm for a dressage concentration. Barbi remembers her experience in training a lovely Trakehner gelding, Rapport. He had the mind, gaits, intelligence, and heart to be a competitive dressage horse. However, his conformation created an obstacle to his being an agile, upper level competitor. His hocks were very straight and as a result, he struggled to attain the essential engagement necessary to perform the demanding exercises required for the more advanced dressage movements. He had to be retired from such work for his overall health and soundness. Now he happily serves as a lower level quadrille competitor and is also ridden by Barbi's daughter Chelsea. He kindly offers her some of the lessons he learned during his dressage education.

Trust reflects our willingness to put ourselves in our partner's hands. We are only willing to do this if we believe in our partner's sense of respect and fairness. Since dressage is based on the slow patient development of the horse, the rider learns to dissect various problems from multiple perspectives. This encourages the rider to set realistic expectations. By following this progression, we only ask of the horse what he is capable of performing. Exercises are utilized to prepare him for each sequential step. As the horse develops through dressage, he becomes more trustworthy. His growing sense of focus, calmness, suppleness and balance

Photo 5 — *A Refreshing Trail Ride.*

Photo 6 — *Majic Focuses on His Work.*

make him a more reliable mount. *(Photo 6, page 7)* In this manner, dressage training improves any horse for any type of riding; trail, hunter-jumper, stock, polo or endurance.

Just as the walls of the pyramid are continuous from the base to the apex, so is the relationship between horse and rider. A solid relationship based on attraction, communication, commitment, enjoyment, purpose and trust underlies dressage at any level. Ultimately, words like "harmony" and "unity" require the coming together of two separate beings, in this case, the horse and rider.

Dressage As Holistic Development

"Many men go fishing all of their lives without knowing that it is not fish they are after."

– Henry David Thoreau

The harmony and unity that we observe in a fine dressage performance reflects the attainment of those qualities on an inner level as well. Several distinct aspects of dressage offer both horse and rider the means to achieve inner harmony. The interconnection between the mind, body, emotions, and spirit or the four sides of our pyramid, has long been recognized and is currently being validated through research. Ancient wisdom from many teachings directs students to integrate the mind, body and emotions in order to achieve spiritual evolution. The revolutionary approach to healing, mind-body medicine, is based on this premise.

> *Intelligence is much more flexible than the mask of matter that hides it. Intelligence can express itself either as thoughts or as molecules. A basic emotion such as fear can be described as an abstract feeling or as a tangible molecule of the hormone adrenaline. Without the feeling there is no hormone; without the hormone there is no feeling.*
>
> *— Deepak Chopra, M.D.*

Many physicians, psychologists, chiropractors, and massage therapists acknowledge that the tissues of our bodies become repositories for our thoughts and emotions. Janet has experienced this mind-body connection while having a massage to relieve lower back pain. While the masseuse worked on the painful area, she began thinking about a miscarriage that had occurred ten years ago. It seemed that her back had remembered this experience. After expressing her sadness, her back pain dissipated. Transplant patients sometimes report strange experiences after receiving a donated heart, kidney or liver. The donated organ apparently releases memories or perceptions into the recipient's body. One heart transplant patient woke up from surgery craving beer and Chicken McNuggets, when she had never desired them previously. It turned out that the donor of the heart was very fond of both. Deepak Chopra concludes that, "Our bodies are made of experiences transformed into physical expression". Given the close connection between our mind, emotions, body, and spirit, it makes sense to develop our awareness of these aspects of ourselves and to help them function more harmoniously.

Mental Development

"The mind leads the body."

– Koichi Tohei

"When we quiet the mind, the symphony begins."

– Anonymous

Dressage disciplines the minds of riders and horses, helping both achieve a higher level of mental functioning. As you may recall, the first side of our pyramid consists of mental development. Riding in harmony requires the rider to put aside all distracting thoughts and focus on each moment of riding. Barbi exhorts her students to "RIDE HERE NOW!" Each time our mind drifts, we must return our attention to the horse. We must let go of the buck that occurred ten seconds ago and return our focus to the present moment of riding. Rather than anticipating that our horse will spook on the long side near the flapping canvas, we prepare by concentrating on each moment that leads up to that moment. By focusing in this manner, we can prevent or resolve the problem, rather than creating or adding to it. If we ride with our minds focused in the present, we can also start each training session fresh, free of expectations based on past experiences. We must connect with our horse and "RIDE HERE NOW!" *(Photo 7)* This degree of focus allows us to pay attention to the smallest details, which helps develop mandatory consistency and desired refinement.

Sharon learned the value of "Ride Here Now" one day while practicing a first level test. She had worked hard on repeated half halts in order to prepare Ariel for each new movement. As she focused on riding each moment stride for stride, Ariel performed beautifully. In her enthusiasm, she became distracted by her success and forgot to prepare for the next movement. Without this preparation, Ariel became stressed and rushed into the canter, above the bit.

Likewise, dressage develops the horse's ability to focus his mind. A horse may express his lack of concentration in many ways. He may break gait, shy, hollow his back, over-react to either surrounding stimuli or the rider, and avoid or abuse soft contact with the bit. Through the correct employment and understanding of dressage principles, the horse presents himself with calmness, patience, and understanding. He filters out distractions and attends to the rider with understanding and soft, immediate responsiveness. *(Illustration D)*

By achieving the horse's attention, focus and confidence, the rider opens a channel of communication through which the horse becomes receptive to

Photo 7 — *Chelsea and Rapport remembering to "Ride here now," moment to moment.*

Illustration D — *Filtering Out Distractions.*

new learning. It is here that the quality of teaching is imperative! We must be aware that whatever we practice, consciously or unconsciously, is what we teach. Inconsistencies in our lessons often create confusion or incorrect learning for the horse. For example, one of Barbi's students became frustrated by her horse's loss of impulsion following transitions. She failed to recognize how frequently any transition became imbalanced by her body falling forward and her legs coming off the horse. She compounded the problem by immediately stopping to talk about it, unaware that her horse viewed stopping as a reward for correct performance. Her frustration was wrongly centered on her horse rather than her own inconsistent behavior.

Because there's so much going on at any given instance, it's highly beneficial to use a coach's feedback to become conscious of our behavior. By riding consciously, we are able to create and better maintain the channel of communication with our horse. When this is achieved, it seems the horse rides off the rider's mind, responding correctly to the slightest of aids. That's when the work is most beautiful.

Physical Development

"When the horse and I are working together not only should it look easy but also it should be easy, for both of us. Only in that way can we both feel happy and satisfied."

– *Kyra Kryklund*

Dressage is both a means and an end to improving physical fitness. Physical development is the second side of our pyramid. Riding dressage supports the four S's of athletic ability as described by Dan Millman in *The Inner Athlete;* **stamina, strength, suppleness** and **sensitivity**. These four aspects of fitness are interrelated. Each contributes an additive effect to the other qualities, as well as a contribution to the whole picture. Dressage provides intense physical exercise, especially in the learning stages. As the horse and rider progress up the tiers of the pyramid, exemplified by the training levels of dressage, the physical demands increase. The training level tests are shorter requiring simple, large patterns performed in the basic three gaits of walk, trot, and canter. Rhythm, relaxation and obedience are paramount. As the team progresses up the tiers to Grand Prix, the tests become longer and more complicated. The exercises demand far greater stamina, strength, suppleness, and sensitivity for both horse and rider.

Duration and intensity offer means to develop **stamina**. To seriously practice dressage, in each training session, we must be willing to push past our fatigue in order to build up our conditioning. Other cross training sports such as hiking, bicycling, dancing, aerobics, etc. enhance our stamina for riding, especially when we only ride two or three times a week. *(Illustration E)* Janet recalls a time before she began working full time, when she would school her horse four times and jog three times a week. After returning to work, she dropped down to riding once per week. In a matter of weeks, she was dismayed when she was exhausted after the first ten minutes

Illustration E — *The importance of cross-training.*

of her lesson. Awareness of our level of stamina helps us to be more effective in training our horse. If we push too far and become tired, then our aids become ineffective. By using a free walk on long rein, we can rest and then return to work replenished. Likewise, the horse also develops increased stamina through intermittent work periods. Care must be taken not to over-stress the horse, by doing too much, too soon. The occurrence of heavy breathing or tripping, lack of willingness, or increased nervous sweating may be signs of over taxing the horse's stamina.

Dan Millman distinguishes between brute strength and **effective strength**. (*Illustration F*) He states that effective strength is "the ability to relax the proper muscle groups while consciously tensing others." He emphasizes this in the following quote, "Greatness lies not in being strong but in the right use of strength." Karolyn at just under 100 pounds gracefully rides Celebrate who tips the scale to 1470 pounds. Obviously, there's something more to this than muscle. (*Photo 8*)

Effective strength in riding is more about when, where, and how we apply our strength. The "when" is about timing. We must first create an opening or receptivity in the horse and then apply the correct aid at the exact moment that permits the horse to produce the desired result. For example, ask for the canter at a specific moment of the stride in either walk or trot. When the horse's inside fore leg carries weight on the ground, use "effective strength," applying the "where" and "how," to maintain a correct body position, and apply clean canter aids. Strength applied at the wrong moment might create a delayed response, resistance, or confusion. In any case, the strength is wasted and the desired result lost. When riders resort to using brute strength, the elegance and harmony so essential to dressage are sacrificed.

For the horse, dressage is a training method designed to gradually develop the horse's correct muscling, enabling him to use his strength more effectively. Horses that have been properly trained show a pretty topline with a well-shaped neck, strong back and hindquarters. *(Photo 9 on page 13)* As the horse progresses in his training, his hindquarters become stronger and more developed to allow greater engagement and collection. An

Illustration F — *Leverage your strength.*

Photo 8 — *Karolyn, a petite rider, demonstrates effective strength.*

improperly trained horse will often exhibit a U neck, in which the muscles on the underside of the neck are overdeveloped.

Suppleness in horse and rider is essential for the horse to develop expressive gaits. Suppleness is characterized by ease of movement, full range of motion in all joints, and increased effective power. A supple body uses less energy in movement. Dan Millman points out the relationship between suppleness and relaxation when he says, "The naturally supple body is a reflection of a relaxed mind." Inevitably, most riders unknowingly carry tension from life events such as physical or psychological disappointments and traumas, which translates into body stiffness. In addition, few of us routinely develop or refine our bodies to perform isolated and fluid movements specific to supple riding. When we fail to acknowledge this, the horse becomes the unfortunate recipient of our tension and stress. It's impossible to expect that we can rectify years of habitual stiffness and tension in the few short hours that we spend in the saddle. Increasing our suppleness is a continual goal in good riding. Stretching out before we ride allows us to become aware of tension and release it. (*Photos 10 and 11*) Monitoring our relaxation while we ride enhances our ability to relax our hips, knees, thighs, shoulders, elbows and wrists, while stretching our upper bodies and dropping our lower legs. Off horse stretching and isolated floor exercises improve our awareness of body

Photo 9 — *Majic demonstrates a well developed topline.*

Photo 10 — *Suraya & Chelsea stretching on the floor.*

Photo 11 — *Suraya & Chelsea stretching while mounted.*

isolation and increase our flexibility. Suppleness serves as a gateway to effective strength. *(Illustration G)*

Dressage training also increases the horse's suppleness. Through trust, the horse develops flexibility, which allows the rider to adjust its body; to bend, straighten, lengthen or shorten its stride and frame. Through years of training and exercise, the horse develops the strength and suppleness to gradually shift its center of balance further back. *(Photo 12A and Photo 12B)* This allows the desired freedom and lightness of the front end, as the hindquarters engage and carry more weight. As a result of this shift in balance, the horse is able to perform with ease the more difficult exercises that are introduced through the stages of training. LaGueriniere recognized the importance of this when he stated:

> *Difficulties have to be overcome by allowing sufficient time to strengthen the horse's muscles. It is this, which makes many think that dressage is pointless. Thus many riders neglect those gymnastic exercises so necessary to achieve suppleness, balance, obedience and collection. Without these exercises, no horse will show good free movements and allow the rider to sit comfortably, regardless of the use to which the horse is put by the rider; fox hunting, jumping, the riding of intricate figures, or all of these pursuits.*
>
> — *LaGueriniere, Paris, 1773.*

Illustration G — Stretching improves suppleness.

Photo 12A — *Sarah's mare on the forehand.*

Photo 12B — *Sarah's mare in better balance.*

Sensitivity in both the horse and rider is essential in achieving the desired harmonious result and is therefore highly valued and sought after. The word sense forms the base of the word sensitivity. Sensitivity can be seen as the opening of our awareness through the five senses. When we "sense" reality, our right- brain is activated and we become fully present in our surroundings. We shift from a left-brain, analytical style of thinking to a more receptive feeling state. Here we experience a oneness with the world around us, including our horse. Most importantly, this state of being, which we access through our sensitivity, is where the horse lives. To meet the horse, we must enter his world. Horses are not analytical thinkers. They deal with the world out of what feels safe and comfortable or dangerous and painful.

Dan Millman further expands the definition of sensitivity in a manner that carries relevance to dressage. His five additional aspects of sensitivity merit further discussion. These senses include the following: *balance,* the ability to detect and correct variance from the vertical; *coordination,* the ability to move different parts of the body independent of one another; *timing and rhythm,* the ability to begin or end a specific movement at a precise moment, and *reflex speed,* the capacity to respond promptly to a particular stimulus.

Dressage riding requires a heightened focus and refinement of balance, coordination, timing, rhythm and reflex speed. (*Illustration H*) If the rider is out of balance, the horse cannot be in balance. The moment a rider sits on a horse, the horse must shift its normal balance to accommodate for the rider's weight. This compounds the necessity for the rider to attain exact balance while riding. This task would be easier if the horse remained stationary! In reality, we can expect a shift in balance moment to moment due to the stride for stride movement of each gait, the changes in the footing, distractions in the environment, and the rider's or horse's stiffness. Maintaining balance becomes further challenged by the expected changes in balance, which occur through changing patterns, movements, transitions within gaits, and levels of dressage training. These facts challenge the conscious rider to continually monitor and adjust his own balance. This skill takes much attention and repetition to become automatic. Riding on the lunge line helps us isolate our attention to balance and serves as an important means to develop this ability. We will discuss lungeing further in Chapter 9. As we advance in our riding skill, perception and correction of imbalance occurs instantaneously.

Balance is a prerequisite for coordination, which is paramount for effective riding. Coordination permits us to apply effective aids, timely corrections and rewards, as well as the ability to move fluidly with the horse. A coordinated rider can move specific parts of the body independently, without adversely affecting other parts of the body. Horses greatly appreciate a coordinated rider. Likewise, as riders, we feel more secure and delighted as we experience the positive results of riding with coordination.

This leads us to the importance of appropriate timing. Horses learn through stimulus response

Illustration H — *We must juggle balance, coordination, timing, rhythm, and reflex speed.*

conditioning. A large part of training involves teaching the horse to yield to pressure. For example, when we teach the horse to yield to pressure, we apply a stimulus of pressure through various means such as closing a leg or touching with a whip. *(Photo 13A and Photo 13B)* Our horse may respond in one of three basic ways; ignore the aid and fail to move, move into the pressure, or move away from the pressure. In this example, the first two responses are undesirable and the third is desirable. Therefore, as trainers, we must immediately correct the wrong response and reward the right response.

The key word here is immediately. Immediately refers both to the start and finish of our response, which conditions the horse's future behavior. Whatever happens immediately following the horse's response to our application of pressure, will be perceived by him as either a reward or a correction. This approach to training requires that we develop reflex speed, which we learn over time through experience. We will discuss specific rewards and corrections in Chapter 10, The Aids. A horse trained with good timing of aids will be more confident, willing, and dependable due to the trainer's clarity. Good timing allows clear training. Round corral work and methods such as "advance and retreat" and "horse whispering" stress the importance of appropriate timing.

Some horses present themselves with a natural good sense of rhythm, as do some people. Occasionally, two such talented individuals may pair up. This is a gift! More often than not, only one or neither of the pair possesses a natural sense of rhythm. Since we're the one carrying the halter and offering this dance, we must take the initiative to develop rhythm for our horses and ourselves. *(Illustration I, page 17)* For the rider, this involves counting the rhythm of the strides. The walk offers four beats; the trot, two beats; and the canter three beats followed by a moment of suspension. Focusing on this improves our awareness of each gait's footfall. Then, we can regulate the horse's rhythm by the following rhythm of our seat. Riding to music or using a metronome can also heighten our awareness of rhythm. Dressage intensely focuses on the development of rhythm, which enhances harmony. The harmony and beauty of musical freestyles showcase the horse and rider's attainment of rhythm.

Photo 13A — *Barbi helping Susanna with leg yield aids.*

Photo 13B — *Susanna performing the leg yield on her own.*

Isabel Werth demonstrated stamina, strength, suppleness and sensitivity in her inspiring musical Grand Prix Kuer at the 1996 Olympics. Her comments reflect the depth of harmony and beauty she experienced that day with Gigolo. She stated, "I had tears in my eyes. It's the best ride that I have ever had on this horse, maybe the best in my life."

Emotional Development

"We don't work with a racket or any other form of sports equipment, but with a living creature that has exactly the same amount of feeling as you."

–Joseph Neckerman

This quote emphasizes the living, breathing nature of riding. As living creatures, both the horse and rider experience a continual flow of emotions that affect performance. Remember that emotional development forms the third side of our pyramid. When we think of emotions, we often judge them as either positive or negative. We've learned this through socialization. We regard happiness and comfort as positive emotions. In growing up, most of us learned that it's acceptable to express these emotions. Therefore, we can allow these feelings to flow freely, creating a sense of relaxation, balance, and well being. In contrast, sorrow, anger, or fear may be viewed as negative emotions. Restrictive messages about expressing these feelings are quite common. After all, "big boys and girls don't cry." Feeling uneasy with sorrow, anger, or fear, adults often deny or suppress these emotions. This creates emotional blockages, which may manifest physically in specific body areas such as tense jaws, constricted throats, tight shoulders and chests, or fluttering abdomens. When we unconsciously hold these "unacceptable" feelings, we create a general physical tension that disrupts the flow of our energy and inhibits our suppleness, fluidity of movement, and open interaction with others, including our horse.

Illustration I — *The rider leads the horse to dancing in good rhythm.*

Dressage provides an arena for examining and choosing to clear these blockages because its essence is based on harmony. Emotional blockages prevent the attainment of such harmony. In order to relate in an intimate, harmonious manner, both our energy and the horse's energy must flow freely, cleared of emotional blocks. Dr. Reiner Klimke spoke of a heightened sense of intimacy when he won the Individual Gold at the 1984 Los Angeles Olympics. He stated, "I have seldom sensed such an intimate connection between horse and rider as I did that day." It would be difficult, if not impossible, to achieve this level of connection and harmony, when we harbor emotional blocks such as fear, anger or resentment. This highlights the importance of assessing our emotional state prior to riding. It is essential that we own our part.

Many people fail to recognize that horses also have feelings. They overlook the importance of acknowledging the horse's emotional state and of building the horse's self-confidence and enjoyment of his work. Horses, like people, possess different types of character. Some are bold, amiable, fearful, defiant, and so on. *(Photo 14A and Photo 14B)* In addition, horses come to us with indelible memory of past experiences with humans. They remember positive encounters, sparse, negative, or confusing interactions. All of these factors influence their emotions. Horses, like humans, can either express or hold their emotions. They may express confusion, fear, or anger through actions such as head tossing, biting, shying, bolting, rearing, kicking, or bucking. Many horses, even at rest, hold tension in their bodies and this tension will be more easily, quickly, or unexpectedly triggered during riding. As with people, stored physical tension disrupts the free flow of energy and inhibits suppleness and fluidity of movement.

Whether the emotions are carried into riding from an outside situation or are generated during our work, the key to dealing effectively with these emotions is acknowledgment. This responsibility lies strictly with the rider, for we possess the reasoning power and the ability to utilize multiple perspectives to understand and resolve the problematic situation. Once we acknowledge the emotion that affects our interaction, we can choose to respond clearly and appropriately, rather than allowing our emotions to dictate inappropriate actions.

On a daily basis, the horse and rider bring their emotional states into each riding encounter. One or both may be in a calm, relaxed mood, paving the way for a harmonious day of riding. However, if one or both feel agitated, angry, or fearful, blockages to smooth interaction may occur. Imagine that a rider is frustrated by family conflict and arrives at the barn feeling tense and irritable. During the ride, the horse fails to pick up the correct lead and the rider explodes in frustration. In this scenario, the rider dumps his previous emotional tension onto the innocent, unsuspecting horse.

Frequently, emotions are generated during our riding encounter. For example, imagine that a plastic bag blows through the arena, frightening a green horse. The horse bucks the rider off. The rider, wanting to impress some onlookers, feels embarrassed and then angry at the horse for causing this awkward situation. Acting out of these emotions, the rider angrily and inappropriately whips the horse. The unacknowledged angry emotional state inhibits dealing effectively with the horse. It fuels a harsh response, aggravating the horse's fear. Had the rider stopped to acknowledge the embarrassment and anger, a more constructive course of action rather

Photo 14A — *If you've seen one horse, you've seen them all.*

Photo 14B — *Don't be fooled for each horse is unique in character.*

than an emotionally fueled reaction could have taken place.

Recognizing our feelings helps us clear our emotional blocks. As responsible riders, we must slow down and turn our attention inward in order to clear previous emotional debris that may prevent effective riding. A variety of methods such as meditation, visualization, or verbal processing can facilitate this clearing. For example, Janet realized that she felt sad and resentful when Aramo's joint block infected his knee, resulting in his premature death. These feelings prevented her from relating to a potential new horse, Sweetness. During her lesson, she felt tense, closed down and unable to focus on Barbi's instructions. She and Barbi took time out to talk about what was going on. Janet recognized her sadness and was able to share her disappointment at the loss of Aramo. After acknowledging this, she was able to separate these feelings from her relationship with Sweetness. Over time, she was able to establish a very clear and appreciative relationship with her new horse.

Acknowledging emotions also applies to the horse. Just as we must slow down and observe ourselves, we also must slow down and observe our horse prior to riding. Our horse's attitude may be affected by multiple variables such as recent work, time of day or month, weather, footing, physical condition, outside distractions, etc. After recognizing our horse's emotional state, we can adapt our work accordingly. This paves the way for more harmonious interaction. For example, if our mare is in heat and hasn't been worked for several days, we may adjust our training session by lungeing or working on suppleness or throughness, rather than introducing a new exercise.

“Your mind will be like its habitual thoughts, for the soul becomes dyed with the color of its thoughts.”

– Marcus Aurelius

In exploring the impact of our emotions on riding, it helps to understand the major role that our minds play in generating our emotions. As a psychotherapist, Janet works daily with her clients to help them understand how thoughts generate emotions. Many people experience their feelings as primary and unalterable. However, when they closely examine what they are saying to themselves, they begin to understand the relationship of thoughts to feelings. As we go about our daily actions and interactions, we continually talk to ourselves. This “self-talk” directly influences how we feel.

Albert Ellis, a psychotherapist and founder of Rational Emotive Therapy, explains that our maladaptive emotions and behaviors are influenced by our negative cognitions. Cognitions refer to our beliefs, attitudes, and perceptions. Usually we remain unconscious of these underlying beliefs and unaware of our “self talk,” responding to it without challenging its validity. Self talk is the inner conversation we hold continually with ourselves. Sometimes this inner dialogue is positive and helpful. Unfortunately, automatic negative thoughts (ANTS) often march in on the picnic and ruin the day. Once we begin monitoring our self-talk, we begin to see that much of what we tell ourselves is illogical. This makes sense because many of our perceptions and beliefs were formed in childhood and often not reworked in adulthood. They remain unchallenged and therefore continue to influence our emotions and actions.

Ellis points out ten major irrational beliefs that commonly lead to anger, self-condemnation, anxiety, fear or frustration. The following seven cognitions especially apply to riding. When we unconsciously believe one or more of the following statements, we generate negative emotions, which can cause physical reactions such as tightness, rigidity, increased heart rate, hyperventilation, slowed reactivity, etc. These physical effects then block effective riding. As you can see, our emotions are not something that “just happen” or that are “out or our control.”

Consider these seven set-ups for blocked progress and see how you might be creating emotional impasses in your own riding.

1. **It is absolutely necessary for me to have the approval and love of everyone.**

When riders believe this statement, it blocks their ability to accept constructive criticism. Barbi recalls an extreme example of this when she gave a lesson to a woman who had difficulty riding a correct circle. Most of the problem was created by the rider's mal-aligned position. During a videotaped lesson, Barbi focused on constructive positional corrections such as inside shoulder back, connection on the outside rein, and maintaining a vertical position. The rider perceived the corrections as disapproval and felt insulted. To defend against these feelings she replaced Barbi's voice on the videotape with Mozart! When the need for approval clouds our ability to listen and learn, our growth is inhibited.

2. **I must be completely competent and able to achieve in all respects if I am to see myself as valuable and worthy.**

Unconscious belief of this statement can adversely affect successful results in competition. Riders who need to prove their value in the show arena may fail to use competition as a means to grow. If achieving in all respects means winning the class, valuable lessons in overcoming obstacles may be overlooked. Showing becomes a miserable arena for proving to the self and others that the rider is a worthwhile, valuable person. For example, Janet worked with one rider, who became very anxious prior to showing. In talking with her, she expressed fear that if she didn't win, her husband would condemn her and her involvement in such a time consuming and expensive sport. She needed that blue ribbon to validate herself and her riding. Just identifying this negative belief helped her relax in the show arena.

3. **My past history is all-important and will continue to strongly affect my life in the same manner as it always has.**

This belief relegates us to the museum of past experiences. Each exhibit, whether of failure or success, keeps us from being fully present in the moment. Riders are particularly apt to make claims such as "I've never been able to keep my seat down," or "My horse always spooks at the judge's stand." As Linda Tellington-Jones explains: "Sometimes the very fact that we expect a certain kind of bad behavior from a horse sets up a self-fulfilling prophecy. The horse reacts to our own tense attitude by mirroring back our expectations." By monitoring your "always" and "never" statements, you can pin point where the past may be impeding your current progress.

One of Janet's clients felt very discouraged about her horse's repeated failure to pick up the canter at the far end of the arena. She was perplexed that this problem didn't occur anywhere else. As they explored this seemingly odd phenomenon, she remembered that once she had fallen off at this spot a year ago. In therapy they worked through this traumatic event. Following this, she was able to focus on her aids without being overly concerned about not getting the correct lead. Soon her horse was consistently picking up the correct lead at this spot.

4. **A perfect or right solution to the problem exists, and it is a catastrophe if I can't discover it.**

Holding this belief, a rider often fails to apply a multi-dimensional approach to problem solving. Instead, one looks for the one magical cure-all. Fred provides an example of the block that this belief creates. His horse violently shied every time he passed the new judge's stand at C. He thought that punishment was the "right" solution to his problem. Many battles later the shying behavior had only escalated. Angry and frustrated that his solution didn't work, Fred pronounced, "I can never ride in this arena again." A more appropriate approach would have been to use a multi-faceted de-sensitization process to minimize the horse's fear. This "solution" would possibly involve various stages over an extended period of time. The rider's patience and openness to multiple, creative solutions may point towards eventual resolution. There is often no single "perfect" solution in riding.

5. If something is or may be fearful or dangerous, I should be very concerned about it and keep thinking about the fact that it will occur.

Ironically this belief often becomes a self-fulfilling prophecy. Horses easily detect their rider's fear and often react adversely. This sets up a negative cycle for horse and rider that seems to reinforce the original dysfunctional belief. One of Barbi's students experienced a breakthrough in her relationship with her horse when she realized this. Kathy's horse was reactive and explosive on a daily basis. As a result, she became increasingly frustrated and fearful. Kathy's tension and fear augmented her mare's tendency to shy, buck and bolt. When Kathy identified her belief that she needed to be worried and focused on disaster, she could adopt a more functional cognition. She decided to tell herself, "She's a hot horse. She may shy or act out, but I can handle it and it doesn't matter." This allowed Kathy to focus on riding to help her horse, rather than fixating on an imagined disaster. As a result, her mare immediately calmed down and acted out less frequently. In Kathy's case, Barbi felt confident that Kathy possessed sufficient skills to back up her new belief that she could handle her mare's acting out. However, if a rider is truly over-faced on her mount, a better solution would be to find a horse that the rider can handle.

6. It is awful when things aren't the way I want them to be.

This belief prevents us from coping with minor and major difficulties. When a problem shows up in our riding, rather than focus on solutions, we become stuck in the "ain't it awful" trap. We complain, shout, or cry rather than deal with the problem. Here we create another problem by telling ourselves that problems are awful. Opportunities to see this belief in action occur daily at most barns and shows. An example of this happened at a horse show, when the judge was delayed three hours by flight difficulties. This caused all of the classes to move back three hours. Riders, who had already warmed up, had to put their horses away and prepare all over again later. Some riders left in a huff, angry at the judge and the show manager. Some complained that their horses would become difficult or cranky. A few looked defeated, as if they had already scored poorly. It's easy to join in this chorus, but doing this can prevent us from coping effectively. One rider acknowledged her disappointment, then chose to view the setback as an inconvenience and decided to use her extra time to her advantage. She massaged her horse and took a short nap in her trailer. This rider avoided the "ain't it awful" trap and instead acted out of a more healthy belief that she could accept unexpected difficulties and deal with them flexibly. *(Illustration J)*

Illustration J — *"It was just one of those bad mane days!"*

7. It is much easier to avoid whatever is difficult rather than to face it.

The chance to skirt around problems rather than deal with them often defeats our riding progress. This belief allows us to find "outs" rather than solutions. Barbi has known riders who back off from necessary training rather than risk their horse's misbehavior. Susan's new horse was apprehensive and unsteady in his contact with the bit. Because he nervously tossed his head, Susan avoided any attempts at maintaining a light, steady contact with his mouth. She feared his tension would erupt in bucking her off. Her avoidance of this problem escalated until she soon avoided even bridling him. Next, she decided to only ride him in a hackamore, which ended her dressage career. Later she sold him to another rider who effectively faced the horse's problem with contact and soon showed him at training level.

Spiritual Development

"Spiritual growth is a journey out of the microcosm into an ever-greater macrocosm."

– Scott Peck

Photo 15 — *Janet experiences connection through meditation.*

The final side of our pyramid is spiritual development. Spiritual growth has been defined in a variety of ways. Most definitions refer to an expansion of self-awareness that puts us in touch with an energy beyond our individual egos. (*Photo 15)* This fosters our appreciation of and connectedness to the universe. Ouspensky, a spiritual mystic, felt that when we free our perception from personal beliefs and bias, we can experience the wonder and magnificence of the world. By simply being with "what is," we open the door to seeing that the magnificence is always present. *In The Road Less Traveled*, Scott Peck describes this interconnectedness ...

> *"The true wonder of the world is available everywhere, in the minutest parts of our bodies, in the vast expanses of the cosmos, and in the intimate interconnectedness of these and all things... We are part of a finely balanced ecosystem in which interdependency goes hand-in-hand with individuation. We are all individuals, but we are also parts of a great whole, united in something vast and beautiful beyond description."*

For Peck, the path of spiritual growth entails discipline and love. Dressage provides a rich and fertile ground for nurturing our spiritual growth. Applying the concepts of discipline and love to dressage, we can better understand how our dressage experience can also contribute to our spiritual growth. Understanding this can also improve our riding.

Discipline involves using four tools: *delaying gratification, accepting responsibility, dedicating oneself to truth,* and *balancing*. (*Illustration K, page 23)* It is well accepted that dressage involves discipline, and is definitely not the sport of choice for someone seeking instant gratification. It is a slow, deliberate, progressive system of training. The rider who embarks on this journey must be able to delay gratification in many ways. First of all, dressage requires a range of time and financial commitment, depending on our goals. In order to focus on and achieve our goals, we are challenged to delay immediate gratification in other areas of our lives. To go up the levels of dressage, we must make riding one of our priorities. It certainly doesn't have to be our exclusive focus, but we must balance and limit our priorities to give our riding justice.

Secondly, there's no predictable timetable in dressage. The horse's ability to develop, as well as the rider's dedication and talent, determine the rate of progress. Sometimes a prospective student asks, "How many dressage lessons will it take for me to become a competent rider." The answer is that it will take as long as it takes. This response stresses the need to *delay immediate gratification* and savor the means, as we patiently and persistently travel toward the end.

Susanna, an eleven-year-old dedicated rider, demonstrates a rider's ability to delay gratification. One lesson, she became discouraged when Sharsea was strong and insensitive to her restraining aids. She was frustrated that she had to give up working on new lessons, in order to focus on quieting him and gaining better control. This required Susanna to be firm and take care of business, rather than wishing he were different. She successfully got through the lesson and later recognized that she had grown a lot that day. She realized that riding wouldn't always feel fun, but that dealing with difficult challenges clears the way for future fun.

To train with a vision informed by wisdom and experience, our agenda must be flexible to meet the individual needs of our horse. Many trainers and riders attempt to prematurely push the horse for immediate results. This often sacrifices harmony, consistency, longevity, and the horse's health. Often the fast way is the slow way!

Finally, the ability to delay gratification means we are willing to work through the present pain to enjoy the future pleasure. Bonnie illustrates this self- disciplined approach to her riding. A naturally stiff rider, she worked through the discomfort of developing her sitting trot by riding without her stirrups daily. Often riders avoid the more uncomfortable exercises necessary to develop a good position in favor of easier, more enjoyable riding time. To reap the pleasurable benefits of dressage, we must often be willing to work through various uncomfortable blocks. Setting personal goals of practicing difficult exercises a few minutes each day develops the strength and coordination to create new habits.

Accepting responsibility involves owning our own part. Often riders blame the horses, their trainers, or the circumstances for problems. Although there may be some truth to these accusations, usually the rider shares in either the creation or maintenance of the problem. Perhaps this means talking out a problem with your trainer, hiring a new trainer, or even choosing a more appropriate horse. Whatever the problem, the responsibility to find the key to the solution rests with the rider.

Dedication to truth involves being open to continual self-examination and challenge. Individuals, by definition, hold a limited perspective. We grow by expanding and adjusting our perspective in reaction to input of others. It's very important to select professional help that enhances the beauty and harmony of our riding and the improvement of the

Illustration K — *The four tools of discipline.*

horse. For example, Ellen worked on her own in dressage and was surprised and concerned when her competitive marks were low. Since she had ridden without feedback for so long, she had failed to correct some basic problems. Fortunately, she sought out instruction and was able to raise her marks by ten percentage points. Dedication to truth solidified her foundation for more advanced work. Dressage offers this opportunity through outside feedback such as receiving instruction and riding tests.

Staying in balance requires flexibility in our judgment. This can be difficult because it involves giving something up, which is one of life's most painful lessons. Our desire to look good, stay in our comfort zone, or win can result in clouded or rigid judgment. To progress in riding, we must maintain our balance in more ways than one. This includes balance in multiple areas such as commitment, goals, beliefs, emotional attitudes, approach to training, etc. Dressage is a wonderful metaphor for balance. The vehicle for learning spiritual balance is there for us if we are willing to transfer the message of dressage to other aspects of our lives.

Love provides the motivation to use these tools of discipline. Peck defines love as "the will to extend one's own or another's spiritual growth." We would alter this definition to include mental, emotional or physical growth as well as spiritual growth. When our interaction with our horse grows out of love, the discipline becomes far less of an effort. This paves the way for increased patience, understanding, and harmony. Love, the willingness to extend ourselves for our horse's development provides a stable and positive foundation for our pyramid of dressage.

Selecting A Trainer

4

> "*Even the Buddha is still working on himself.*"
>
> – *Anonymous*

This quote emphasizes the importance of lifelong growth and learning. Even internationally acclaimed riders are still working on themselves. Selecting an appropriate trainer is one of the most important decisions you will make, equaling that of choosing your horse. An effective trainer assesses and guides the rider's and horse's mental, physical, emotional and spiritual development from the base of the pyramid to the pinnacle.

The relationship with your trainer plays a significant role in both horse and rider's progress. (*Illustration L)* A trainer's "eyes from the ground" provide a keen, discriminating perspective for seeing both correct and incorrect movements. It is far easier to correct an incorrect position or aid immediately, before it becomes an engrained habit. The relationship between you and your trainer allows you to utilize this knowledgeable feedback. The ACCEPT model, introduced in *Chapter 2, "Why Dressage,"* can also help you assess your relationship with a current or potential trainer. Recall the ACCEPT model explained on page 4 addresses the Attraction, Communication, Commitment, Enjoyment, Purpose, and Trust involved in relationships.

Attraction provides the initial draw toward a certain trainer. When Barbi and Janet observed Dr. Reiner Klimke and Biotop at the Los Angles World Cup in 1995, the harmony and grace were evident. As always Dr. Klimke seemed to ride effortlessly and Biotop responded in a light and happy manner. The pair obviously enjoyed performing dressage. The crowd clearly agreed and the applause in time with Biotop's steps filled the auditorium. When observing a trainer, it is paramount that you would like to model yourself after this equestrian.

Communication that is clear, direct and responsible allows the rider to grow without humiliation. Sometimes uncomfortable lessons are hard to

Illustration L — *A constructive, positive team.*

swallow, such as those regarding "your part" in the situation. Yet to progress as riders, we must be willing to confront these challenges. A trainer must be able to communicate criticism constructively. Constructive criticism focuses on precise instruction regarding behavioral changes that a rider must make. Attacking a rider's character could create shame and a feeling of inadequacy. Barbi has occasionally heard students repeat hurtful comments made to them by other trainers. Even if these harsh criticisms were motivated by attempting to spur a student's growth, they often lower a rider's self esteem and could even cause a rider to quit riding completely. A trainer with good communication skills can guide you and your horse through limitations and challenges in a manner that promotes success and pride.

A good trainer can also receive communication non-defensively and respond appropriately. When a rider brings up a grievance or a difference, the trainer should be able to hear the student fully and consider the student's viewpoint seriously. When the trainer doesn't agree with the student, an explanation of the trainer's reasoning is given clearly and respectfully. Mutuality and respect ideally underlie all interactions between students and trainers.

Illustration M —
Observe the picture portrayed by your perspective trainer and mount.

A trainer's **commitment** to dressage and to teaching dressage can be assessed in several areas. A broad understanding of horse behavior, good horsemanship, appropriate progression of training and good dressage implementation should be demonstrated by the trainer.

How can a rider assess these qualifications? Fortunately, you don't have to do this on your own. Trainers who compete show a willingness to submit themselves and their horses for inspection by a qualified dressage judge. The trainer should either presently or previously have competed successfully in at least your level or above. If you have the opportunity to watch a trainer compete, notice the picture presented by the pair. *(Illustration M)* The general picture should radiate pride, polish, preparation, and harmony. While judging a show, Barbi observed a trainer enter a competition with an unkempt appearance. Her horse was dirty, had an unclipped rangy coat and straggly long mane. The rider's coat was unbuttoned and her hair was messy. She talked throughout the test, going off course three times. Her low scores reflected her lack of preparation and inappropriate demeanor. As in all professions, trainers range from poor and incompetent to excellent and highly competent. Checking out a trainer's competition record can help you distinguish where your potential trainer lies on this continuum.

Commitment to teaching is also important. You can learn a lot by talking to a trainer's students. Learn how long they have been with the trainer and how far they have progressed. Observe their attitudes towards their horses, the trainer and other students. Notice how the majority of students ride. In general, does their riding reflect their trainer's emphasis on correct position? In Europe the importance of correct position to good riding goes unquestioned by the masters. There are no short cuts there! At the Spanish Riding School in Vienna, the young riders live on the lunge line for months or even years, before they are allowed to take the reins or stirrups. Such an emphasis needs more stress in this country.

If some of the students compete, notice the outcome. Find out if their scores have improved over time. Riders do not have to be advanced to demonstrate that they have been exposed to the basics. As all seasoned competitors know, it takes many times of making mistakes in competition before a polished, successful ride is predictable. A compassionate, effective trainer offers technical and positive emotional support to guide students along the challenging road to success, both in and out of the competition arena.

Enjoyment of riding and teaching should be obvious when observing the trainer. A general positive outlook enhances enthusiasm for learning. Does the trainer "light up," smile, laugh and seem to enjoy working with horses and students? Do the students express an overall enthusiasm for their trainer and for dressage? Remember this sport is supposed to be fun! *(See Photo 16)*

Purpose varies among trainers and should be clarified and compared to your purpose. Some trainers are openminded and experienced in working with any type of horse and level of student. Their versatility is apparent when watching a day's worth of lessons. Other trainers seek only upper level competition type horses and students with well-developed ability and experience. Barbi has often heard the complaint that "a previous trainer had nothing good to say about me or my horse." For this reason, discuss the specifics of your situation and goals with a trainer to check for compatibility.

In searching for the right trainer for you and your horse, you must decide if you want to turn your horse over to the trainer, or if instead you want to be supported to do the riding yourself. Often Barbi talks to riders who wish they could do more riding, but their trainer refuses to let them ride their own horse. Sometimes this may be a safety issue. On the other hand, it may be a trainer's practice to compete on the horse personally to attain higher scores. Discuss this issue with your trainer to reach a mutually satisfactory decision.

Trust involves the trustworthiness of the trainer both as a person and as a professional. Check out the reputation of the trainer by talking to a variety of people who have had dealings with this person. A person of integrity is usually regarded highly by his or her community, friends and family.

A professional trainer can be trusted with the safety of both students and horses. Find out about the track record of accidents, both human and equine, as well as safety procedures followed at the barn. Sometimes accidents don't involve the trainer. Other times a trainer may have over-faced a rider, pushed a rider or horse too quickly, used unsafe tack, or failed to maintain a safe environment.

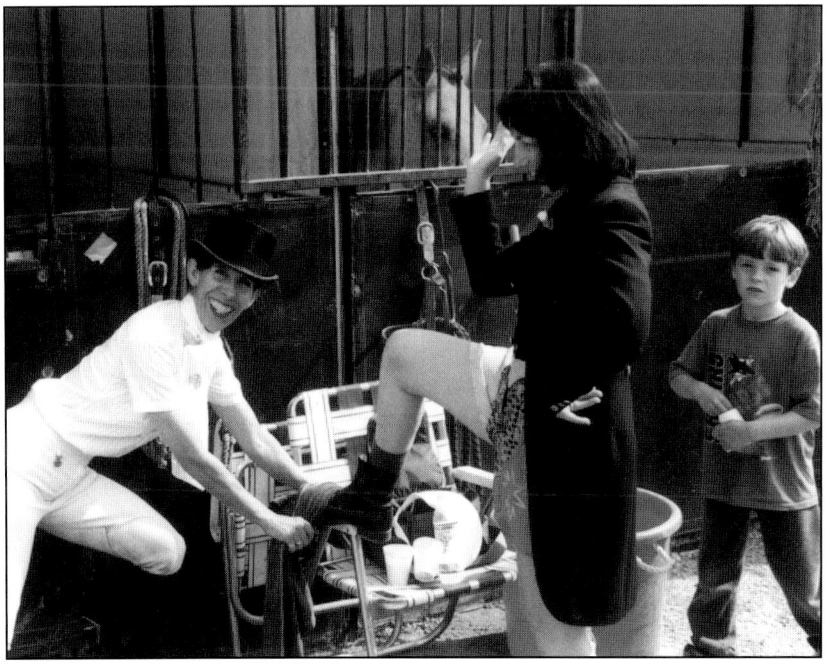

Photo 16 — *Switching roles, Barbi and Janet share a lighter moment at the show.*

A professional trainer possesses the credentials necessary for the type and level of instruction he or she performs. Credentials can be earned from experience and performance in training and competition or from recognized training programs such as the USDF Instructor's Certification.

Finally, a professional trainer is motivated by a desire to enhance the horse and rider's growth. When this conflicts with the trainer's desire or need to make money or enhance a reputation, the reputable trainer resolves this conflict in the best interest of the students and/or horses. Avoid trainers that allow personal agendas to interfere with student or equine progress.

By using the **ACCEPT** model to choose a trainer or evaluate an existing relationship, you can enhance your riding context. Even in the best of trainer/ student relationships, the time may come when you outgrow your trainer. If you choose to select a new trainer, let your current trainer know of your plans. This communication honors the role your trainer has played in your progress. How you end the relationship with a trainer can either extend appreciation and acknowledgment to your trainer or send a message of disregard and lack of appreciation.

5

What is: Assessment of Rider And Horse

"*Most problems precisely defined are already partially solved.*"

– Harry Lorayne

Mental awareness and clarity help us address the many interacting factors necessary for a constructive riding experience. By assessing the present situation of both the horse and rider, we are able to realistically and effectively plan our equestrian goals. This involves analyzing where each horse and rider are in terms of the nine levels of the pyramid from the foundation of training level to the highest pinnacle of Grand Prix.

Hilda Gurney, Olympic rider and internatonal judge, explains that, "It is wise to have short & long range goals in mind for each horse you ride. These goals do vary… depending on each individual's level of training and experience." She begins each training session with a "basic blueprint," which may be adjusted according to the horse's mental and emotional needs. Such clear and flexible goal setting is equally important for the rider.

Ancient Wisdom

The following Japanese story humorously reminds us that analyzing the situation prior to action results in the most rewarding outcome.

An old Samurai warrior knew his time on earth was near an end and wished to bequeath his sword to the brightest of his three sons. He designed a test. He had a friend hide just inside the barn, above the doorway, and gave him three bags of rice. He then invited each son inside, one at a time. The first son, after feeling the rice bag fall on his head, drew his sword and cut the bag in half before it hit the ground. The second son halved the bag even before it hit his head. The third son, sensing something amiss, declined to enter the barn- and so earned his father's sword.

Frequently we are like the first son, planning after the fact, and therefore fail to avoid the negative consequences. Falling in love with the horse's beauty or playing rescuer may cloud our ability to see the realistic unsuitability of purchasing a particular horse. This could result in being "hit over the head" with a negative outcome like an injury or such extreme difficulty that we give up.

Sometimes, we resemble the second son, who partially assesses the situation, and therefore prepares to meet the problem. This may occur when we fail to see all the important variables of the riding situation. For example, Janet purchased Request, a yearling paint filly, for her high school daughter as an affordable future prospect. She assessed the filly's soundness by having a vet check to confirm conformation and health. Since she could lead, groom, bathe, and tie the horse without problems, she determined that her daughter would be able to safely handle her. However, she failed to assess Request's willingness to be caught. Ironically, this yearling had been caught by roping and fled in fear from human approach. Like the second son, Janet avoided being hit on the head by determining the problem early on and hiring a ground trainer, who worked with her for several months to facilitate haltering Request more easily.

If we are wise, we are like third son, who sees that something is up and avoids the problem completely. The more clearly we assess all aspects of our riding experience, the less problematic this experience will likely be. It is wise to extend our assessment abilities by hiring the experienced eyes of riding instructors, veterinarians, and horse trainers. Recently Pam obtained a vet check on an Arab/Quarter cross that she had been leasing and showing successfully for a year. The vet noted some soreness in the high suspensory tendons and recommended against purchase because of the horse's poor conformation of the lower legs. This conformation put the horse at risk for injury as the work increased. With the vet's input, she declined purchase and very likely avoided the sadness and disappointment of future predictable lameness.

Past and Future Inform the Present

By looking honestly at their current situation and riding goals, riders can achieve more effective and timely results. Sometimes we prefer to create a fantasy rather than to face an uncomfortable reality. Yet both rider and horse pay a price for denying the reality of "what is," by feeding unrealistic expectations. First we must assess our riding commitment, which is influenced by our past, present and future.

What is our riding history? Have we grown up at ease in the saddle, with wishful dreams fed by fiction, or with nightmare experiences on a rental horse? Previous positive, educated and successful interaction with horses serves as a sound basis for continued progress. Uneducated previous experiences with horses tend to feed our blindness about "what is" now. For example, fond memories of riding gentle, "bomb proof" horses may lead to false security in the present. Barbi often hears "I know how to ride," only to discover that this student's unfounded horsemanship portends an accident waiting to happen. *(Illustration N)* Vicarious experiences through movies or novels coupled with a love for horses may provide motivation, but without education, can be dangerous. Negative past experiences may have resulted in dislike or fear of horses. These attitudes may be overcome with patience and perseverance in the context of a progressive, supportive, supervised program. Our history greatly influences our commitment and our goals.

Our future, as envisioned by our riding goals, also impacts the present. Many riders choose a horse before clearly formulating their goals. Yet, a clear idea of our goals can help us make a wiser choice in the present. There are many methods of achieving our goals from a simple, direct route, to a round about detour into the forest. Either route is okay, provided we understand the implications of our

Illustration N — *An accident waiting to happen.*

choice. By understanding our goals and matching temperaments of horse and rider, we can use the variables introduced in this chapter to construct a road map for reaching our destination more directly. Some riders are very clear about their riding goals. Others have never really thought about goals, other than having a general goal of riding or owning a horse. One method of formulating our goals involves active imagination. Janet often helps her clients see their goals by asking them to imagine being interviewed in three years. You can tape record the following text in a slow, calm voice, allowing time for you to execute each instruction. Then go through your own guided visualization in order to define your riding goals.

Close your eyes and turn your attention inward. Slowly allow your body to relax. Beginning with your head, notice any tension in your facial muscles. See that melt away. Allow your shoulders to become warm and heavy, dropping whatever burdens you are carrying. Take a deep breath in, expanding your chest fully. Now exhale. Relax your abdomen, buttocks, thighs and feet. Feel your entire body become heavy and warm.

Imagine that it is three years from now. You have accomplished something in your riding that you feel very proud of. As you look into your inner visual field, you can see yourself performing this accomplishment. When your visualization is complete, open your eyes.

For the individual who has difficulty with visualization, you can vary this by imagining that someone is interviewing you about your recent riding success. Then listen to what you are saying to the interviewer.

Now write down any ideas that came to you through this process. Perhaps you only saw a starting point for further study, or maybe you envisioned a more detailed picture. In either case, your inner guidance can help you begin to define your riding goals. Use any ideas that come up for further investigation and clarification. Then discuss these ideas with your trainer. (*Illustration O)*

By realistically assessing the past and envisioning clear future goals, we can make a more informed, workable choice in the present. Assessing the present involves looking at a number of variables, which affect the degree of our commitment and the nature of our equestrian plans. The rider's variables include: expertise and knowledge, level of assertiveness and confidence, physical fitness, athletic ability, maturity and emotional stability, available time, finances and family support, proximity to trainer, and goals. The horse's variables include age, size, soundness, temperament and trainability, athletic ability, training, fitness, conformation, gender, cost, and availability. By looking at how the rider's and horse's variables interact, we can predict the smoothness of the match. More importantly, we can identify areas of poor fit and create plans to enhance the match.

For example, Chuck, an inexperienced, non-rider, who loved horses, was given a Swedish Warmblood foal, Blazer. This illustrates an extreme mismatch,

Illustration O – *Envisioning One's Goals.*

with horse and rider at polar ends of appropriateness. Such a match will require a high level of commitment, which involves much time, energy, money, guidance, and family support. Chuck did possess this intense commitment and created and carried out a comprehensive plan that gradually over five years resulted in a successful fit. He learned groundwork from a trainer weekly and practiced these lessons with Blazer for three years. He also read books and watched videos on training. In addition, he began weekly riding lessons on a school horse with Barbi. He was willing to invest considerable time and money to this pursuit and enjoyed the support of his wife to accomplish this goal. In addition, he had a realistic goal of being able to ride Blazer within five years. Chuck enjoyed the challenge and process of growing, bonding, training, riding and eventually competing at training level with Blazer.

If the fit between horse and rider is poor and commitment is lacking, a poor end result can be expected. The stories of winning a free Arab abound! Frequently, the recipient is a child, whose parents have no knowledge of horses, and the Arab is an unruly yearling. (*Illustration P*) In this case, going against the adage and "looking the gift horse in the mouth" constitutes wisdom. By realizing that our commitment doesn't meet the requirements of the fit, we bypass many problems. On the other hand, by assessing "what is," a closer if not perfect match can be selected. Jenny, one of Barbi's seven-year old students, wanted a horse of her own. Her parents committed to spending a set amount of time and money to support Jenny to become a safe equestrian. After extensive looking, Barbi located an older, quiet, willing Quarter Horse mare named Sheba. Sheba perfectly matched Jennifer's needs. They developed a deep bond and enjoyed years of safe riding, practicing the lower levels of dressage. Since the fit was initially so close, a less intensive and comprehensive plan was needed in order to maintain the commitment required for a successful outcome.

Illustration P — *The Gift horse.*

Wendy provides another example of the importance of careful assessment of "what is" in order to create a realistic, successful plan. A relatively green rider, with limited funds and two hours per week to devote to riding, she identified her goal as slow, progressive improvement towards riding training level dressage. Acknowledging her limited time and money, she decided to lease a quiet, well broke horse and take one group lesson per week and an occasional private lesson. The close fit between her lease horse and her ability and experience enabled her limited plan to work. She achieved her goal of making gradual progress as a training level rider.

Through knowledgeable and honest assessment of the fit between horse and rider and the desired goal, we can predict the extent and intensity of the riding program needed to achieve success. A number of variables are impacted by the nature of these two factors. As stated previously, finances, time, degree of involvement in a training program for horse and rider, physical condition and fitness, and family attitudes influence the outcome. By taking the following questionnaire, you can determine the nature of fit between your selected horse and yourself in order to see "what is."

Notice below that the rider's expertise and the horse's training are compared to the stages of dressage training: walk trot, training level, 1st level, 2nd level, 3rd level, 4th level, Prix St. George, Intermediare I, Intermediare II, and Grand Prix. These ten levels, which form the ten steps of our pyramid, allow a more accurate assessment of the rider and horse's dressage effectiveness. In the other areas it may be helpful to associate the number value with the labels that correspond to dressage scores. Later we refer to scores from 1-4 as low, 5-6 as medium, and 7-10 as high.

Experience and expertise as a rider overall can strongly affect the rider's score. A true horseman will most likely score high for rider, even though they have only ridden training level dressage. The reverse situation is also possible. Previous experience in hunt or saddle seat may have formed habitual adaptations of the rider's position that may be difficult to change. The key for determining the effect of previous riding experience seems to lie in the rider's flexibility and adaptability. Therefore use both your judgment and your trainer's assessment to arrive at a meaningful score.

1	2	3	4	5	6	7	8	9	10
very bad	bad	fairly bad	insufficient	sufficient	satisfactory	fairly good	good	very good	excellent

Assessment of the Rider

1. Expertise (numbers = level)

W/T*	Tr*	1st*	2nd*	3rd*	4th*	PSt.G*	I_1*	I_2*	GrPx*
1	2	3	4	5	6	7	8	9	10

2. Knowledge

1 2 3 4 5 6 7 8 9 10

(not knowledgeable) … (very knowledgeable)

3. Assertiveness and Confidence

1 2 3 4 5 6 7 8 9 10

(timid) … (assertive)

4. Physical Fitness

1 2 3 4 5 6 7 8 9 10

(weak, poor stamina) … (strong, high stamina)

5. Athletic Ability

1 2 3 4 5 6 7 8 9 10

(stiff, lacks sensitivity) … (supple, sensitive)

6. Maturity and emotional stability

1 2 3 4 5 6 7 8 9 10

(immature, irrational, reactive, defensive) … (very mature, rational, stable)

**Walk/trot, Training, 1st., 2nd., 3rd., 4th., Prix St. George, Intermediare 1, Intermediare 2, Grand Prix*

7. Available Time

1	2	3	4	5	6	7	8	9	10

(very limited, 1-2 hours per week) — (as much as it takes)

8. Available Finances

1	2	3	4	5	6	7	8	9	10

(very limited) — (unlimited)

9. Proximity to trainer or instructor

1	2	3	4	5	6	7	8	9	10

(unavailable) — (available)

10. Family Support

1	2	3	4	5	6	7	8	9	10

(lack of support) — (high level of support)

11. Goals (numbers = level)

W/T*	Tr*	1st*	2nd*	3rd*	4th*	PSt.G*	I_1*	I_2*	GrPx*
1	2	3	4	5	6	7	8	9	10

Assessment of Horse

1. Age

1	2	3	4	5	6	7	8	9	10

(very young: 2-3 or older 20-25) — (peak years: 5-19)

2. Size

1	2	3	4	5	6	7	8	9	10

(does not suit rider) — (suits rider)

3. Soundness

1	2	3	4	5	6	7	8	9	10

(chronic lameness) — (very sound)

4. Temperament and trainability

1	2	3	4	5	6	7	8	9	10

(hot, unwilling) — (calm, willing)

5. Athletic ability

1	2	3	4	5	6	7	8	9	10

(uncoordinated, stiff, poor gaits) — (coordinated, supple, 3 good gaits)

6. Training (numbers = level)

W/T*	Tr*	1st*	2nd*	3rd*	4th*	PSt.G*	I_1*	I_2*	GrPx*
1	2	3	4	5	6	7	8	9	10

**Walk/trot, Training, 1st., 2nd., 3rd., 4th., Prix St. George, Intermediare 1, Intermediare 2, Grand Prix*

7. Fitness

1	2	3	4	5	6	7	8	9	10
(very poor condition or health)									(healthy and in good condition)

8. Conformation

1	2	3	4	5	6	7	8	9	10
(poorly conformed)									(well conformed for dressage)

9. Availability

1	2	3	4	5	6	7	8	9	10
(lesson horse, rarely available)				(lease)					(owns)

10. Gender

1	2	3	4	5	6	7	8	9	10
(does not suit rider)									(suits rider)

11. Cost

1	2	3	4	5	6	7	8	9	10
(not affordable)									(affordable)

**We advise obtaining a pre-purchase exam from a qualified veterinarian to evaluate soundness and conformation. The cost is well worth knowing whether or not this horse is suitable for your intended purpose.

Red Flag Variables

Several variables serve as red flags to disqualify the match for the majority of riders. Certain disorders of temperament and soundness can create a dangerous riding situation. Infrequently, horses possess an inability to be domesticated. These horses lack an ability to bond with and trust human handlers and are often unpredictably reactionary and explosive. Even experienced, effective trainers may decline purchasing such a horse. Other horses learn a defiant temperament and continually challenge the trainer's requests. Seriously consider if you can train or hire a trainer to deal with this type of horse.

Bonnie answered an add for a "quiet kid's horse." On mounting the horse for a trial ride, the horse suddenly froze and began to shake. Bonnie jumped off, only to be reassured by the seller that the horse had never done this before. He excused the horse's behavior by saying that he hadn't been ridden for some time. She observed the horse on two more occasions without seeing the freezing behavior. Bonnie purchased the horse for her children. To her dismay, she saw numerous repeats of this behavior, inexplicably triggered, in the following weeks. Care was taken to rule out a condition termed "cold-backed," in which a horse may react violently when girthed too tightly, then mounted too quickly. The saddling and mounting process was taken very slowly with intermittent periods of walking. The behavior rapidly escalated to rearing and falling over backwards. Amazingly, no one was injured! Later, after a western trainer futilely worked with this horse, it was humanly put down. Stories abound that have a more tragic ending than this, due to a poor evaluation or disregard of temperament disorders.

Soundness disorders can also create a danger to safety, making the choice of such a horse unwise. The following scenario illustrates this hazard. Ann owned a large, 1800 pound Warmblood named

Hogan. She hoped that through dressage training, Hogan would learn to balance his bulky frame and uncoordinated way of going. She sought the assistance of an experienced trainer and spent several months working on exercises designed to improve his weak areas. Rather than improving over time, Hogan's imbalance increased to the point of periodic episodes of ataxia and falling down. A vet examined Hogan and agreed with the trainer that the horse's ataxia created a hazardous riding situation and recommended that the horse be turned out permanently to pasture. Sadly, Ann's love for Hogan clouded her judgment and she continued to ride him lightly. Shortly thereafter, a disastrous accident occurred in which Hogan suddenly lost his balance and fell on Ann, almost taking her life. Fortunately, she recovered and made the necessary decision to end Hogan's riding career.

Highly Influential Basic Variables

The following variables heavily affect the attainment of certain riding goals and the parameters of the training program. These variables deal with the most basic factors for the rider and horse. For the rider, we will assess scores for expertise, knowledge, physical fitness and athletic ability. For the horse, we will evaluate scores for conformation, training, athletic ability and temperament/ trainability.

Example 1: An experienced Trainer and Green Horse

Barbi, a Grand Prix rider, and Majic, a green broke training level five-year old served as our first example. We entered the following scores for this pair:

Barbi: expertise 10, knowledge 9, physical fitness 8, athletic ability 8.

Majic: conformation 10, training 2, athletic ability 5, temperament & trainability 5.

These figures showed a high scoring rider (all scores from 8-10) and a mixed scoring horse (scores ranging from 2-10). A more advanced rider can effectively train a horse with minimal training, undeveloped agility and less willing temperament and can improve these three areas through training.

In expertise, we gave Barbi a 10 because she is a Grand Prix level rider. She has earned a bronze, silver, and gold medal with United States Dressage Federation and has been listed with the United States Equestrian Team several times. In terms of knowledge, Barbi rated a 9 because she has trained a number of green horses to Grand Prix level, some of them lacking natural talent. Her philosophy to always "remain open to additional learning" was enhanced by her challenges while training many types of horses. For physical fitness, Barbi scored an 8 because she exhibited the stamina and strength to train 4-6 horses a day and dance ballet and jazz weekly. We subtracted 2 points due to her small frame and limitations in strength due to previous injuries. She received an "8" for athletic ability. She integrates stretching exercises through her day and possesses a high degree of body isolation awareness and ability. We subtracted 2 points due to previous back and neck stresses, which necessitate riding with greater care to preserve her suppleness. Barbi's total score of 35 reflected a highly skilled rider, capable of training a green horse. Yet, her profile also pointed to her need to protect her back and neck by eliminating very strong or rank horses.

Majic illustrated a low scoring horse due to his youth and lack of training. Importantly, for Barbi, he scored a "10" on conformation and was highly suitable for dressage work. We scored him generously at a "2" for training level because he could walk, trot, and canter, but was basically green broke. He scored a "5" for athletic ability because, although he naturally possessed a good walk and canter, his trot was flat with little use of his back. In addition, he was clumsy, having little awareness of his feet. He received a "5" for trainability/temperament. Initially his temperament was somewhat suspicious, which created a shorter fused, sullen attitude. However, when approached tactfully, he became open to learning and grew in confidence and trust. His scores indicated a horse that needed a tactful and extensive training program to reach his innately high potential.

The strength in this match was carried by the rider. In this case, the match worked because the rider possessed the skill to develop Majic's weak areas. Importantly for Barbi, Majic had excellent dressage potential and an acceptable score of "5" for temperament/trainability. Any score lower than "5" in this area would expose Barbi to unacceptable risk for stress or injury. Therefore, this match was workable. Through the gradual implementation of dressage training, Majic's weak areas could develop to produce a beautiful dressage team. Indeed, a year later, in 1995, this team produced consistent scores of 70% at first level, winning Champion Holsteiner at First Level for the United States. By the age of 10, he was trained to Grand Prix.

Example 2: A Beginning Rider and a Schoolmaster

Conversely, a high scoring horse may serve as a schoolmaster for a low scoring rider. When Janet began riding in 1986, she purchased Des, a fourth level, kind schoolmaster, to learn dressage. The following scores illustrate this pair.

Janet: expertise _1_, knowledge _5_, physical fitness _6_, athletic ability _6_.

Des: conformation _10_, training _6_, athletic ability _8_, temperament/trainability _10_.

Janet grew up riding western with little supervision, but was familiar and comfortable with horses. She was taking lunge lessons, when Des became available for sale. Barbi encouraged her to purchase Des as a schoolmaster.

As a walk/ trot level rider, she scored a "1" for expertise. In terms of knowledge, she rated a "5". She had been involved in her daughters' dressage lessons and had helped groom, tack, and lunge their horses. In addition, she took bi-weekly instruction, had attended Barbi's weekend riding seminars, read books, and watched dressage videos. She also observed safety guidelines in her riding. Her score of "5" in physical fitness revealed that as a novice, she had sufficient strength and stamina to begin. Moreover, she recognized that she must develop these qualities to improve her riding. She rated a "5" in athletic ability because of her previous athletic history of swimming and gymnastics as a young person. However, she needed to develop her suppleness and sensitivity for riding. Her scores illustrated a beginning rider with definite potential. Her strong commitment to receiving dressage instruction helped increase her effectiveness as a rider.

Des provided a good example of a school horse. His conformation score of "10" revealed that he was well suited for dressage work. His training scored a "6" for fourth level. His athletic ability rated an "8," with 2 points deducted for a string halt condition that affected his gait, causing him to lift his left hind leg somewhat higher than the right hind. Finally, his temperament and trainability were a "10." This horse was very forgiving, honest, and reliable. His high scores showed that he would be able to perform well as a dressage schoolmaster. In evaluating this match, we see that the rider had much to learn and that the horse was capable and willing to assist her. Indeed, within a year, Janet's dedication and Des's generosity of spirit created a team that successfully rode at first level.

Self-Assessment

Enter your scores for the following:

Rider: expertise _____ , knowledge _____ , physical fitness _____ , athletic ability _____

Horse: conformation _____ , training _____ , athletic ability _____ , temperament & trainability _____

The following questions will help you evaluate the interaction between rider and horse scores in order to analyze the compatibility of your match.

Look carefully at your scores and answer the following questions:

1. Given my expertise and knowledge what type of horse would best suit me?

____

2. Given my physical fitness and athletic ability, what type of horse would best suit me?

____

3. Given my horse's conformation and training, what type of rider best suits him?

____

4 Given my horse's athletic ability and temperament/trainability, what type of rider suits him?

____

Assessment Conclusions

1 Carefully think about and write down one sentence that most clearly states your dressage goals.

____

2. Look at the availability of a trainer and your resources and commitment to working with a trainer. State how much help, money, and time (considering work and family) you can realistically allocate per week for your training program.

____

3. Realistically evaluate the interrelation of your personality (assertiveness and confidence) with your experience and compare it with the personality of your horse. Now describe the weaknesses or strengths that show up in your match.

____

4. Decide whether or not your horse and rider match will work with the above underlying factors. Describe the strengths that your match possesses.

____

Our system of assessing "what is" can be applied to purchasing a new horse or re-evaluating your approach to a currently owned horse. If you are in the market for a horse, assessment of these variables will clarify your search, saving you time, money and frustration. For a currently owned horse, assessing these variables can help you adapt your current training program to address weaknesses and capitalize on strengths. Finding the right match or enhancing the current match paves the way for a more harmonious partnership.

6

The Rider's Position

"The rider must first get things right in their body and then just go with the horse."

– *Conrad Schumacher*

Recall that the relationship of the rider and horse is like the inner and outer sides of our pyramid's wall. Before we move up the tiers of the pyramid, we must acknowledge the rider's leadership role in maintaining a strong wall. If the rider's inner wall crumbles due to a faulty, imbalanced, or tense position, the horse's outer wall of correctness, balance, and receptivity will reflect this weakness.

Before working to improve the horse's gaits, we must first focus on the rider's position. This is because the horse is greatly influenced by how the rider sits. When a rider sits in a balanced posture, maintains a supple lower back, and allows the horse's movement to flow smoothly through his body, the horse has the greatest chance to walk, trot and canter in a calm and even manner. When a rider sits in a crooked fashion, such as collapsing one hip, throwing one shoulder forward, or bracing the feet against the stirrups, the tension and lack of balance will be quickly transmitted to the horse. In response, the horse often reflects the rider's poor position by jigging, hollowing the back, or moving with crookedness, irregular rhythm, or uneven steps.

"When the lowest vertebrae are plumb erect,
The spirit reaches to the top of the head.
With the top of the head as if
Suspended from above;
The whole body feels itself light and nimble."

– *The Classics of Tai-Chi-Ch'uan*

Mirror Mirror On The Wall: Assessment of Body Basics

The following two exercises are designed to be performed in front of a mirror or window, which casts a visible reflection. They will promote awareness of body alignment and placement. By seeing any habitual lack of symmetry in your body alignment, you can acknowledge "what is." With this awareness, you can make a commitment to correct it. This process may be difficult and uncomfortable, as habits are often hard to change.

1. Stand on the ground with slightly bent knees, your legs spread about two and a half feet apart, and your toes facing straight ahead. Now drop your hips and seat bones evenly. Allow them to feel heavy.

Then as your torso stretches upward, lift your rib cage off of your hips and press your shoulders back and down. Gently lengthen your neck out of your shoulders with your ears level and your head balanced over your shoulders. Feel the straightness of your spine as your ears, shoulders, hips and heels form a straight line. You should also notice a vertical line from the point of the knee to the tip of the toe. Now turn sideways to check for this alignment.

2. Sit astride the horse facing the mirror, with your horse's head and body facing forward. *(Photo 17)* Now evaluate the evenness of your head carriage, your shoulders, your ribs, your hips, your seat bones, your legs, and your feet. Allow your upper arms to hang softly down slightly ahead of the side seams of your shirt. While looking at your image, make the necessary corrections so that your body is indeed straight. Zip up an imaginary zipper from your belly button to your chin. Then take a deep breath and relax into this corrected, straight position, without collapsing. Now turn your horse sideways and recheck your body alignment. Also check to see that your lower arms form a direct line from your elbow to your wrist to the horse's bit. You might find that as you correct one part of your body, another part may return to an incorrect placement. This is to be expected. Keep working on this, as it is through awareness and constant repetition that new, correct habits will replace old, incorrect ones.

All change is inherently uncomfortable. We can expect new body positions to initially feel incorrect. This discomfort lets us know that we are actually making changes. If we are willing to endure the discomfort, we eventually break through to a new and greater feeling of ease in our riding.

In order to solve the puzzle of a correctly placed, effective position, we'll take apart the various pieces of the puzzle, which comprise the individual body parts. Metaphors provide a simple, concise picture to help students master the basics. Many trainers use word pictures to emphasize various skills. *(Illustration Q)*

1. Plug in your Seat bones to the power source.

Your seat bones serve as your electrical power source, connecting your energy with that of your horse. To stay plugged in, they must bear your

Photo 17 — *Jessica evaluating her alignment.*

Illustration Q — *The individual pieces fit together well with a correct position.*

weight. Although the weight distribution may vary slightly according to the movement ridden, the connection of both seat bones must be maintained. This facilitates what the Germans refer to as Durchlassigkeit. In Dressage Insights, Kathy Connelly defines Durchlassigkeits as the "uninterrupted flow of energy from the hind end forward, and returning from the front to the hind end." Anne Gribbons adds that "It is maintained by keeping a consistent connection between the horse's mouth and the rider's hand at all times, thus keeping the energy that is generated from the rider's leg and seat flowing from the hocks through the back and mouth of the horse in an uninterrupted circle-like fashion."

Your hips influence the placement of your seat bones. If your hips tilt backwards or forwards, sideways or become frozen, your seat bones will lose their fluid connection and effectiveness. Be sure your seat bones are placed in the middle and deepest part of the saddle. Adjust your seat in the saddle so that your weight feels and looks evenly distributed. If one side of your body feels contracted or sunken, lift the arm of that same side straight over your head. At the same time, stretch that leg long and down the horse's side.

Uneven seat bones often stem from rigidity in the hips. To increase hip flexibility, you can perform isolation exercises while on the ground. Dance, aerobics, yoga and stretching on the floor all promote greater hip mobility, which enhances a balanced seat that leads to supple riding. Barbi has witnessed dramatic improvement in students who have engaged in alternate activities to become more supple and agile. (*Note*: see Chapter 7, Floor Exercises.)

2. Stretch your upper body along a vertical beam of light.

Imagine a beam of light entering the top of your head and traveling along a vertical line down your spine and down into your seat bones. Carry your upper body along this vertical plane, neither ahead nor behind it, as this will negatively affect the horse's balance. When you are balanced on the vertical, your horse has the best chance of reflecting this balance by moving with ease.

As a correction, lean slightly ahead of the vertical, then slightly behind the vertical. This helps train your kinesetic awareness and muscle memory to identify the vertical or 12:00 noon position. If your weight falls ahead of the vertical, the horse may react by either speeding up or slowing down. For a beginning rider, feeling a horse continually rushing ahead can be quite intimidating. The most common error of pulling on the reins, with the weight thrown forward, while bracing the feet, amplifies the horse's response of rushing ahead. Some horse's react to the rider's imbalance with additional tension and fear. Too often, in the next sequence of events, the rider becomes fearful or angry and blames the horse for disobedience. In reality, the horse was set up to produce this undesired result. Unfortunately, misunderstanding, lack of trust, disharmony, and a more severe bit are often the consequence.

If the rider's weight shifts behind the vertical, he falls behind the horse's movement, again, negatively affecting the balance. Often the rider compensates by pulling on the reins, which dulls the horse's mouth over time and may evoke fear, unnecessary tension and hollowing. Sitting behind the vertical may also be misinterpreted as a driving aid, causing the horse to surge forward. The resulting lack of clarity undermines the harmony of moving with the horse in perfect balance, rhythm, and flow.

In stretching upwards along the vertical beam of light, avoid hollowing your back and tilting onto your pubic bones. While remaining stretched, relax into this position without sagging the lower back. Often when working on the upper body, riders loose their seat, which provides a base of support. Remember that your seat in the saddle can be compared to a tripod with the weight evenly dispersed between the two seat bones and the pubic bones or fork. In this position, allow your stomach and buttocks muscles to relax.

3. Project a bright beam of light up and out of your chest.

Let it shine up and out as you elongate your neck and press your shoulders back and down. This facilitates the chest remaining uplifted and your upper body energy moving up and out. The horse will reflect your up and out energy by moving more lightly forward in balance. This upper body carriage is especially important for collection, mediums, and extensions. Lifting the chest allows the lower back and hips to move independently of the rest of the body, which also improves the sitting trot.

While uplifting your chest and pressing your shoulders back and down, keep your shoulders level. Imagine that your collarbones are a carpenter's level and the bubble of the level is in the middle of your throat. Keep the bubble level all the time. When you forget to maintain evenness in your shoulders, your body will attempt to compensate for the lack of symmetry farther down with uneven hips, seat bones and legs. Once again, the rider's unevenness in the saddle will negatively affect the horse's way of going.

Your shoulders should always line up with your horse's shoulders. When traveling on straight lines, your shoulders remain straight. When circling or turning, in order to align your shoulders with your horse's shoulders, your inside shoulder must rotate slightly back to allow the turn. A very common fault occurs when the rider leads with the inside shoulder. As a direct result, the horse cannot turn smoothly. The rider's mal-aligned shoulders block the horse's ability to follow the desired shape or direction. The circle becomes a squared off shape, often accompanied by the horse rushing, leaning in, and hollowing, due to the inhibited balance and blocked direction. Sometimes, the horse responds by leaving the shape or desired direction completely, only to be reprimanded for following the rider's inaccurate body aids. Frequently, the rider attempts to correct this situation by pulling the horse's nose around to the desired direction. However, the rider's inaccurately placed shoulders and lack of outside rein and leg outweigh this feeble attempt to control the horse.

Photo 18 — *Karolyn demonstrates an exercise for improving body rotation on a circle.*

To correct the habit of leading with the inside shoulder, place your inside arm behind your back, keeping your forearm parallel to the ground. *(Photo 18)* Holding your reins in the outside hand, ride the circle, turning your horse with your remaining aids. Notice that with properly aligned shoulders, your horse can turn now that you've gotten out of his way. Often horses respond by moving more happily, relaxed and better stretched. Another valuable corrective exercise is for the rider to repeatedly look back to the horse's inside hind hip. The resulting slight twist in the torso repositions a faulty shoulder alignment.

Once you have corrected your shoulder placement, you can use the following exercise to maintain your shoulder alignment while executing correct circles. Place a cone in the middle of a 10 to 12 meter circle. Hold the reins in the outside hand and point to the cone with the inside hand. Now ride the circle repeatedly in walk, trot, or canter. You'll realize that it takes many repeated corrections to maintain your body position and ride the correct shape. It is humbling to realize that riding a correctly scribed circle is not as easy as one might think. Barbi reminds her students "Be there, or be Square!"

4. Balance a book on the top of your head.

This image will help you carry your head straight and level. Your head weighs close to twenty pounds. Imagine the effect of twenty pounds pulling your body off center as it cocks either forward or sideways. Usually the body will compensate for this distortion by collapsing the shoulders or hips.

If your head tips forward, the book will land in your lap, your shoulders will tend to collapse and your upper body will come in front of the vertical, tilting your seat bones forward. To correct this, reach the head and neck back towards the collar of your shirt.

If your head tips sideways, the book will slip to the ground, the inside shoulder will drop, and the inside hip will collapse, compromising the evenness of your seat bones. This causes two possible problems: the horse and rider may fall in on their shapes or the horse might pop his outside shoulder, leaving the shape. To help correct this, imagine that you are wearing a heavy earring on the opposite higher ear, and elongate the collapsed side.

Balancing a book on the top of your head will help you achieve the uplifted carriage so important to an effective and elegant position.

5. Use your eyes like bifocals to enhance your dual vision

Dressage riding involves dual vision. Your peripheral vision allows you to be aware of your surroundings and plan your direction of travel. At the same time, you must focus your eyes softly forward on the horse's poll area. This allows you to evaluate such issues as proper flexion, correct carriage of the poll, straightness in alignment, use of correct muscling and throughness. You can also observe the correct use of your hand aids until the correct feel is mastered. However, in either type of vision, your eyes should not become fixed or glazed as this can create a hardness and rigidity in the overall effect of the application of the aids.

6. Envision a constant current of life energy flowing though your arms, hands, legs, knees, and feet.

From the moment you sit astride your horse, you must receive the horse's energy through a supple, relaxed, and balanced body. Any gripping, stiffness, bracing and imbalance immediately block this flow of energy. This blockage creates an immediate tensing reaction somewhere in the horse's body. Klaus Balkenhol, USET dressage coach, stresses the interchange between horse and rider. He states, "The horse is a mirror, reflecting how the rider is sitting and what he is feeling." *(See Photo 19)*

Too often, riders forget that their arms and hands connect directly to the horse's mouth through the reins. The importance of remembering this cannot be overly stressed. By acknowledging and respecting the sensitivity of the horse's mouth through correct usage of arm and hands, you can preserve the natural lightness and sensitivity of your horse's mouth. All riders appreciate riding such

Photo 19 — *Celebrate mirrors Barbi's supple, balanced position.*

a horse. Dull mouths are not born. They are trained through the incorrect usage of the hands.

Allow your upper arms to hang softly down from your shoulder. The vertical placement of your upper arms should be slightly ahead of the side seams of your shirt. Your elbows remain flexed and responsive, creating an imaginary line from the elbow through the hand to the bit. This angle will vary as the horse's head stretches to the correct placement for his level of training. In all gaits, the rider's upper arms, elbows and hands must respond to the horse's natural flow of movement.

Close your hands in a soft fist with your thumbs facing upward, as though holding a coffee mug. The thumb presses the rein against the forefinger. Close your fingers on the reins. This allows for a responsive hand and prevents rein slippage. Your wrists must remain supple and pliable, able to flex in, up, or down as needed. Supple wrists permit a soft, elastic contact to be established with the horse and appropriate hand aids to be administered.

Your legs must be carried directly under your seat in order to achieve balance, flow of energy, and placement for effective application of aids. Remember that an imaginary line begins at your ear and passes through your shoulder and hip and ends at your heel. This places you in a vertical position, as though you were standing on the ground with your legs about two and a half feet apart. It takes time for your ligaments, tendons, and musculature to adapt to correct leg placement. As mentioned earlier, body stretches off the horse and lungeing exercises, while mounted, can assist greater flexibility. A relaxed, correctly placed leg allows subtle, accurate leg aids, which creates a calm responsive horse.

Relax your thighs and stretch them long and down the saddle. Avoid pinching your thighs, as this conveys tension to the horse. Feel your thighs hanging fully down from your hip joints, without arching or collapsing the small of your back. Imagining that your thighs have air under them, may help you relax them. Often when the rider relaxes the thighs, the horse immediately relaxes. If your thighs are too loose, falling away from the saddle, you must close the gap to eliminate space between the upper leg and the saddle. Balance between muscle relaxation and tension must be reached.

Keep your knees relaxed and not gripping. When the knees tighten, tension is relayed to the horse. Tight knees interfere with the ability to maintain the lower leg close to the horse's side, and may lighten the depth of the seat. When riders feel insecure in the saddle, they frequently tighten their knees. Ironically, this protective response frequently augments a difficult or scary situation. Feeling the rider's tension, the horse may rush forward, become unsteady, or even buck.

Allow your lower legs to stretch down like wet towels, close to the horse's sides. Only the actual weight of the leg and foot rests in the stirrup. Avoid shoving your heels down against the stirrups, as this conveys tension to your horse. Your heels should be only slightly lower than your toes because the majority of your weight is carried in your seat, not in your heels. Place the ball of your foot on the stirrup with your foot resting on the outer portion of the stirrup. Your toes should point straight ahead.

7. Soften all the joints of your body with warmth so that they become pliable like modeling clay.

Your joints must remain joints. This means that they must sustain flexibility and suppleness at all times. The five major joints that must remain pliable are the elbows, wrists, hips, knees, and ankles. In the walk, follow the horse's neck motion with your elbows. Your hips and hands will move in opposition, like an accordion player's hands. When the hands follow forward, the hips follow back. When the hands follow back, the hips follow forward.

In the rising trot, allow your elbows to open and close so that your hands remain low and quiet. To establish this movement while posting, hook your forefingers under the front of the saddle pad. This allows awareness of the subtle movement the elbows must make during posting when your hands are held still at a constant place. Let go and check to see if you can maintain this resulting quiet hand placement. In the sitting trot, your elbows remain quiet, allowing a steady, quiet contact with the horse's mouth.

In the canter, the elbows subtly follow the horse's neck movement, more or less, depending on the horse's level of training. The movement of the hands and hips go together, both moving forward and back simultaneously. Check your wrists by looking down to see if they are locked and fixed. Supple wrists move more subtly and effectively in applying rein aids. Bouncing in the saddle reflects stiffness in the hips. Floor exercises, mounted exercises, and hooking two fingers onto the pommel of the saddle while riding assist in teaching the hips to follow the horse's movement. Check to see if your knees are locked, by looking down to see if your lower leg is straight and forward. If so, bend the knee and bring the lower leg back so that looking vertically down over your knee, you can only see the tip of your toe. Check your ankles to see if they are locked or if your feet are braced or turned out. A supple or springing ankle will slightly flex with the movement of the horse. To release ankle tension, circle the ankles up, in, and down. For the rare rider who toes in, circle the ankles up, out, and down. For increased ankle flexibility, you can also stand up on your stirrups, push up onto your toes, and then let your heels sink downward. Repeat several times.

Illustration R — *The ongoing conservation of sending and receiving.*

Sometimes it is necessary to brace against the horse with your back muscles, still your body, or close your hand into a fist. Even then, avoid becoming brittle or stiff. This allows the horse to accept the restraining aids more cooperatively without added complications created by your stiffness.

8. Conduct an invisible, active conversation by connecting your mind and body with that of the horse.

A dressage conversation is an in-depth discussion, not a casual chat. *(Illustration R)* This requires you to fully focus on the inevitable moment-to-moment changes that occur between horse and rider. Like all good assertive communication, the dressage discussion is clear, consistent, fair, and mutual. In *Your Perfect Right,* Michael Emmons and Robert Alberti state that assertive communication is based on the communicator's desire to respect and be respected by the receiver and to work out a solution. As explained in *Chaper 10, The Aids,* an assertive rider speaks **clearly** by giving accurate, non-conflicting aids; **consistently**, by repeating corrections and rewards in a timely fashion; **fairly**, by taking responsibility for setting the horse up for success; and **cooperatively**, by immediately noticing and rewarding positive response to the aids. Rewards include a moment of lightening the contact, a soft word, a pat on the neck, or a short walk and rest. Focused, assertive communication produces quiet, harmonious interaction between horse and rider.

In contrast, the passive communicator gives in to the receiver out of fear of conflict. Likewise, the passive rider avoids any potential conflict with the horse. As a result, the horse becomes spoiled and unruly, if not dangerous. To the other extreme, the aggressive communicator often augments conflict and tries to win by overpowering the receiver. Similarly, the aggressive rider, out of anger or lack of sensitivity, often invites conflict and uses unfair tactics to power the horse into submission. The horse may oblige, but often with resentment, resistance, fear, or loss of spirit.

These students all demonstrate good positions.

Stretch Towards Supple Riding: Floor Exercises

7

> *"The object of stretching is to open and free all joints, depending upon the demands of your favorite activities. You'll feel an ease of movement ... You'll also extend your range of power."*
>
> – *Dan Millman*

The second side of our pyramid, physical development, stresses the importance of the four S's; stamina, strength, suppleness and sensitivity. Although all are essential to effective riding, this chapter especially recognizes the need for developing suppleness. Most of us have given up daily vigorous exercise by the end of our teenage years. In addition, we experience daily stress, which can create muscle contraction, stiffness and crookedness. As a result, our bodies lack the suppleness and the ability to perform isolated movement, so necessary to effective riding. Since riding involves continual movement of both the horse and rider, the rider's suppleness or rigidity directly affects the horse's performance. The supple rider enhances the horse's ability to move freely and happily. A stiff rider frequently blocks the horse's movement, creating frustration and resentment. In order to give clean, clear aids, the rider must be able to isolate various body parts.

The following stretches, demonstrated by Suraya and Chelsea, will increase both suppleness and the ability to isolate selected parts of the body. These exercises can be performed at any time of the day. However, when executed immediately prior to riding, they will create greater relaxation and suppleness for your ride.

We've included exercises to stretch and supple all parts of the body that typically affect riding; neck, shoulders, ribs and waist, hips, sides, legs, thighs and hamstrings. There are forty-six exercises in all. You can tailor your stretching program by choosing the exercises you need most, or by selecting a couple from each area. Depending on your needs and available time, you can create a more extensive or a more limited stretching program.

Photo 20 — *Neutral Position*

Stretching Safely

Please take the following precautions in order to avoid injury.

1. Consult your physician or sports trainer regarding possible limitations due to injury or body structure, prior to attempting these stretches.
2. Become familiar with each exercise before trying it.
3. Use a mirror or a partner to confirm correct posture for each exercise.
4. Perform the stretch slowly, extending each stretch only to your own level of comfort.
5. Hold each stretch to a slow count of five.
6. Listen to your body. Stop a particular exercise if you experience pain.
7. Start slowly. Increase the range and hold of the stretch and the number of repetitions gradually according to your judgment.

Photo 21A —
Neck Stretches, Head to Right

Neutral Position *(Photo 20)*

Many of the exercises begin and end with the balanced riding position. We refer to this as neutral.

1. Stand erect, spine straight and head facing forward.
2. Shoulders level and pressed down.
3. Knees slightly bent and shoulder width apart.
4. Toes point straight ahead.
5. Arms rest at your sides.

In this position, an imaginary line beginning at the ear would line up with the shoulder, hip and heel.

Photo 21B —
Neck Stretches, Head to Left

Neck Stretches

When riders relax their necks, often their horses blow out, indicating relaxation.

Right and Left

1. Stand in neutral.
2. Turn your head to the right. *(Photo 21A)*
3. Hold 5 counts.
4. Return to neutral.
5. Turn your head to the left. *(Photo 21B)*
6. Hold.
7. Return to neutral.
8. Repeat 5 times.

**Remember to keep your head properly aligned as in neutral.

Down and Up

1. Stand in neutral.
2. Lower your head, chin tucking towards the chest. *(Photo 22A)*
3. Hold.
4. Bring your head back to neutral.
5. Raise your head back, lifting up out of your shoulders, eyes looking up at the sky, as your chin lifts. *(Photo 22B)*
6. Hold.
7. Return your head to neutral.
8. Repeat 5 times.

**Avoid dropping your head back like a heavy weight. Keep your shoulders evenly pressed down.

Photo 22A — *Neck Stretches, Tucking Chin*

Side to Side

1. Stand in neutral.
2. Tip your head to the right side, gently pressing your ear towards your right shoulder. *(Photo 23A)*

**Avoid raising your opposite shoulder.

3. Hold.
4. Return your head to neutral.
5. Tip your head to the left, gently pressing your ear towards your left shoulder. *(Photo 23B)*
6. Hold.
7. Return your head to neutral.
8. Repeat 5 times.

Photo 22B — *Neck Stretches, Lifting Chin*

Out and In *(Photo 24)*

1. Stand in neutral.
2. Reach your head and neck forward, (like a turtle reaching out of its shell).

Photo 23A — *Neck Stretches, Head Tipped Right*

Photo 23B — *Neck Stretches, Head Tipped Left*

Photo 24 — *Neck Stretches, Chin Out and Back*

3. Hold.
4. Return to neutral.
5. Reach your head back. Picture your neck reaching toward the back of your collar.
6. Hold.
7. Return to neutral.
8. Repeat 5 times.

**Be sure to keep your shoulders and body in alignment, allowing only your head and neck to move.

Photo 23A — *Neck Stretches, Head Tipped Right*

Head Roll, Side to Side

1. Stand in neutral.
2. Tilt your head to the right, gently pressing your ear towards your right shoulder. *(Photo 23A)*

**Avoid raising your opposite shoulder.

3. Gently roll your head from the right, chin tucked, down to center, *(Photo 25)* continuing to the left shoulder. *(Photo 23B)*
4. Gently repeat, slowly rolling your head left to right, in the same manner.
5. Repeat 5 times.

Photo 25 — *Neck Stretches, Chin Tucked, Head Center*

Shoulders

Shoulder relaxation and isolation affects the rider's alignment to the horse and the horse's alignment to the shapes and movements being performed. When the rider's shoulders are crooked or rigid, they adversely affect correct circles, corners, serpentines, lateral movements, and the horse's overall straightness.

Shoulder Press

This exercise helps correct the habitual forward roll, which our shoulders tend to develop as we perform many activities with rounded shoulders and heads dropped.

1. Stand with your back against a wall.
2. Align your head, shoulders, hips and heels to the surface of the wall.
3. Press your shoulders against the wall as you lift your chest.
4. Hold for 5 counts.
5. Repeat 5 times.

Photo 23B — *Neck Stretches, Head Tipped Left*

Elbows Back

This exercise teaches a forward placed, mis-aligned shoulder to stay back in a correctly held position. It is also very valuable performed while mounted.

1. Stand in neutral.
2. Place the right elbow behind your back, keeping the upper arm close to your side and your lower arm horizontal to the ground. *(Photo 26)*
3. Hold.
4. Repeat with the left elbow.

***Variation*: Both arms may be folded behind your back at the same time, to help teach both shoulders to stay back.

Photo 26 — *Shoulders, Arm Behind Back*

Up and Down

1. Stand in neutral.
2. Lift your right shoulder upward toward your right ear. *(Photo 27A)*

**Keep your left shoulder properly aligned in neutral.

3. Hold.
4. Press it back through neutral and then down. *(Photo 27B)*
5. Hold.
6. Repeat with your left shoulder.
7. Repeat 5 times each.

Photo 27A — *Shoulders, Right Shoulder Lift*

Forward and Back

1. Stand in neutral.
2. Press your right shoulder forward. *(Photo 28A)*

**Keep your left shoulder properly aligned in neutral.

3. Hold.
4. Press your right shoulder through neutral and back. *(Photo 28B)*
5. Hold.
6. Repeat with your left shoulder.
7. Repeat 5 times each.

Photo 28A — *Shoulders, Right Shoulder Forward*

Photo 28B — *Shoulders, Right Shoulder Back*

Photo 27B — *Shoulders, Right Shoulder Down*

Photo 27A — *Shoulders, Right Shoulder Lift*

Photo 27B — *Shoulders, Right Shoulder Down*

Forward, Up, Back and Down

1. Stand in neutral.
2. Press your right shoulder forward. *(Photo 28A)*
3. Hold.
4. Press your right shoulder up towards your right ear. *(Photo 27A)*
5. Hold.
6. Press your right shoulder back. *(Photo 28B)*
7. Hold.
8. Press your right shoulder down below neutral. *(Photo 27B)*
9. Hold.
10. Repeat with your left shoulder.
11. Repeat 5 times each.

**Keep opposite shoulder level in neutral.

Photo 28A — *Shoulders, Right Shoulder Forward*

Photo 28B — *Shoulders, Right Shoulder Back*

Shoulder Roll

1. Stand in neutral.
2. Perform previous exercise with your right shoulder in a continual roll.
3. Repeat with your left shoulder.
4. Repeat 5 times each.

Shoulder Roll – Arm Extended

(Photo 29A, 29B)

1. Stand in neutral.
2. Perform the above exercise with each arm extended, right and then left.
3. Repeat 5 times each.

Photo 29A — *Shoulder Roll, Arm Extended Up*

Photo 29B — *Shoulder Roll, Arm Extended Back*

Arms Back

1. Stand in neutral.
2. With arms straight, clasp your hands behind your back. *(Photo 30A)*
3. Lift arms back and up.

**Maintain your vertical alignment, as in neutral.

4. Hold.
5. Repeat 5 times.

Arms Back Variation

From step 3 in Arms Back:

4. Bend forward from your waist and lift your arms behind your body, as far as is comfortable. *(Photo 30B)* Bend knees for further stretch. *(Photo 30C)*
5. Hold.
6. Release.
7. Repeat 5 times.

Arm Presses to the Side *(Photo 31)*

1. Stand in neutral.
2. Using your left hand, press your right arm to the left, horizontally across your chest.

** Avoid lifting your shoulders.

3. Hold.
4. Repeat with your left arm.
5. Repeat 5 times each.

Arm Presses Behind Head

1. Stand in neutral.
2. Reach right arm upward to the sky.
3. Bending right elbow, drop hand to touch your shoulder.
4. Place left hand on your right elbow and gently press backward. *(Photos 32A, 32B)*
5. Hold.
6. Repeat with your left arm.
7. Repeat 5 times each.

Photo 30A — *Shoulders, Arms Back*

Photo 30B — *Shoulders, Arms Back Variation*

Photo 30C — *Shoulders, Arms Back Variation*

Photo 31 — *Arm Press to Side*

Photo 32A — *Arm Press Behind Head*

Photo 32B — *Arm Press Behind Head*

Photo 33 — *Rib Side to Side*

Ribs and Waist Isolations

Ribs and waist isolations increase body awareness for coordination and suppleness. These stretches help create a more flexible seat, which increases the ability to sit well without bouncing.

Ribs Side to Side *(Photo 33)*

1. Stand in neutral.
2. Press only your ribs to the right.

**Keep your shoulders level and your hips over your feet.

3. Hold.
4. Return to neutral.
5. Press your ribs to the left.
6. Hold.
7. Return to neutral.
8. Repeat 5 times each.

Photo 34A — *Rib Press Back*

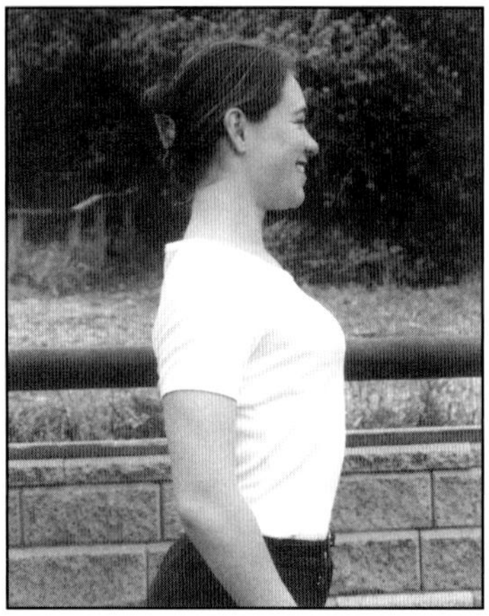

Photo 34B — *Rib Press Forward*

Ribs Right, Back, Left and Forward

1. Stand in neutral.
2. Press your ribs to the right. *(Photo 33)*
3. Hold.
4. Press your ribs to the back. *(Photo 34A)*

**It's as if someone is pushing a fist into your stomach.

5. Hold.
6. Press your ribs to the left. *(Photo 33)*
7. Hold.
8. Press your ribs to the front. *(Photo 34B)*

**It's as if someone is pushing you from behind.

9. Hold.
10. Repeat 5 times.
11. This exercise may be repeated to the left.

Ribs Circled Smoothly

In this exercise, you will draw a circle with your ribs. Press into each point of the circle (right, back, left and front) smoothly, without hesitation.

1. Stand in neutral.
2. Press your ribs to the right.
3. Press your ribs to the back.
4. Press your ribs to the left.
5. Press your ribs to the front.
6. Repeat a smooth circle 5 times.
7. Reverse the exercise, beginning to the left.
8. Repeat 5 times.

Refer to photos 33, 34A and 34B on page 54.

Photo 35 — *Ribs Pressed Forward and Upward*

Rib Contractions: Right Angle Position

1. Stand in front of a support such as a counter or bar.
2. Bend forward from the waist and rest your arms on the support. *(Photo 35)*

**Your torso will form a right angle to your legs.

3. Press your ribs downward.

**Only press until you feel a stretch.

4. Hold.
5. Contract through your stomach, as you press your ribs upward.
6. Hold.
7. Repeat 5 times.

Photo 36A — *Hands and Knees, Press Ribs Down*

Rib Contractions: Hands and Knees Position

1. Position yourself on your hands and knees.
2. Press your ribs downward. *(Photo 36A)* Your back will appear swayed.
3. Hold.
4. Contract your stomach and ribs upward. *(Photo 36B)*
5. Hold.
6. Repeat 5 times.

Photo 36B — *Hands and Knees, Press Ribs Up*

Photo 37 — *Hips Right / Left*

Photo 38 — *Hips Back / Front*

Hip Stretches

Hip stretches contribute to coordination, range of motion, and suppleness. These three factors improve the ability to follow the horse's movement smoothly.

Hips Side to Side

1. Stand in neutral, with knees slightly bent.
2. Press your hips to the right. *(Photo 37)*

**Keep your shoulders level.

3. Hold.
4. Return to neutral.
5. Press your hips to the left. *(Photo 37)*
6. Hold.
7. Return to neutral.
8. Repeat 5 times.

Hips to the Right, Back, Left and Front

1. Stand in neutral.
2. Press your hips to the right. *(Photo 37)*
3. Hold.
4. Press your hips to the back. *(Photo 38)*
5. Hold.
6. Press your hips to the left. *(Photo 37)*
7. Hold.
8. Press your hips to the front. *(Photo 38)*
9. Hold.
10. Repeat 5 times.

Hip Circles

1. Stand in neutral, with knees slightly bent.
2. Press your hips to the right.
3. Press your hips to the back.
4. Press your hips to the left.
5. Press your hips to the front.

**Make the circle as smooth and continual as possible, keeping the shoulders level.

6. Repeat 5 times.
7. Reverse the exercise to the left and repeat 5 times.

Hip Stretches: 2:00, 4:00, 8:00, & 10:00 o'clock

This exercise can be helpful in clarifying the canter depart aid. Think of a clock with the center directly under your seat. 12:00 would be directly forward of your pubic bone.

1. Stand in neutral, with knees slightly bent.
2. Press your hips forward and to the right to the 2:00 o'clock position, while lifting the right heel. *(Photo 39A)*
3. Hold
4. Return to neutral.
5. Repeat 5 times.
6. Press your hips back and sideways to the 4:00 o'clock position. *(Photo 39B)*
7. Hold.
8. Return to neutral.
9. Repeat 5 times.
10. Press your hips forward and to the left to the 10:00 o'clock position, while lifting the left heel. *(Photo 39C)*
11. Hold.
12. Return to neutral.
13. Repeat 5 times.
14. Press your hips back and sidways to the 8:00 o'clock position. *(Photo 39D)*
15. Hold.
16. Return to neutral.
17. Repeat 5 times.

**This sequence may be performed in any order, as learning to differentiate the different positions teaches suppleness and coordination.

Photo 39A — *Hips Stretch Forward and Right*

Photo 39B — *Hips Stretch Back*

Photo 39C — *Hips Stretch Forward and Left*

Photo 39D —*Hips Stretch Left and Back*

Hip Arcs: Half Circles

1. Stand in neutral, knees straight.
2. Press the hips to the right. *(Photo 40A)*
3. Press the hips in a continuous arc to the front, center position. *(Photo 40B)*
4. Press the hips in a continuous arc to the left. *(Photo 40C, page 58)*
5. Reverse the arc from left to right.
6. Repeat 5 times.

**Notice the stretch in the front of the hips.

Photo 40A — *Press Hips Right*

Photo 40B — *Arc Forward / Center*

Photo 40C — *Hips Press Left*

Photo 41 — *Hips Lift*

Photo 42 — *Hip and Shoulder Stretch Kneeling*

Photo 43 — *Hip Stretch Standing*

Hip Stretches: Lying on Back

1. Lie on your back, with your feet on the floor and knees bent about shoulder width apart. Rest your arms by your sides.
2. Lift your hips upward, balancing your weight on your shoulders and feet. Let your head rest on the ground. *(Photo 41)*
3. Hold.
4. Repeat 5 times.

Hip and Shoulder Stretch: Kneeling

1. From a hands and knees position, stretch backward while your arms reach forward. *(Photo 42)*
2. Hold.
3. Repeat 5 times.

Hip Stretch: Standing, Legs Crossed

1. Stand in neutral position and cross your right leg in front of your left leg.
2. Bend your knees a little further, placing your hands on your crossed leg for support. *(Photo 43)*
3. Press your hips further to the left side, feeling the stretch in your left hip.
4. Hold.
5. Repeat 5 times.
6. Repeat the exercise to the right side.

Hip Stretch: Lying Down, Legs Crossed

1. Lie on your back, feet on the floor about shoulder width apart with knees bent.
2. Cross your right leg over your left knee. *(Photo 44)*
3. Lift up on your left leg, until you feel the stretch in your right hip.
4. Hold.
5. Repeat 5 times.
6. Repeat the exercise with your left leg crossed over the right, 5 times.

Hip Stretches: Squatting

1. Stand in neutral with legs more than shoulder width apart.
2. Bend forward, keeping your back flat, and press your knees out with your elbows. *(Photo 45A)*
3. Hold.
4. Return to neutral.
5. Repeat 5 times.

**Variation:* Position the toes out and rock gently from side to side, while pressing the knees out with the elbows. *(Photo 45B)*

**Keep your back as flat as possible.

Photo 44 — *Hip Stretch Lying Down, Legs Crossed*

Lateral Side Stretches

Lateral side stretches not only feel good, but also help increase suppleness and range of motion. These exercises help reduce stiffness, which inhibits flexible riding.

Lateral Stretch: Neutral Position

1. Stand in neutral.
2. Reach arms over your head and clasp you hands together.
3. Stretch arms to the right, until you feel a nice lateral stretch. *(Photo 46A)*
4. Hold.
5. Repeat to the left.
6. Hold.
7. Repeat 5 times.

**This exercise can be adapted *(Photo 46B)* to give additional support as you stretch to either side by holding onto something. This helps support the back and stomach muscles, until they are stronger.

Photo 45A — *Hip Stretch Squatting*

Photo 45B — *Hip Stretch Squatting, Toes Out*

Photo 46A — *Lateral Stretch From Neutral*

Photo 46B — *Lateral Stretch With Arm Support*

Photo 47 — *Lateral Stretch With Forward Bend*

Lateral Stretches: Forward Bend

1. Stand in neutral.
2. Clasp hands together in front of you.
3. Bend forward, while pulling stomach in.
4. Reach to the right side, with your arms stretched out in front of you. *(Photo 47)*

**Keep hips facing straight ahead.

5. Hold.
6. Stretch slowly through center to the left, again with arms stretched out in front of you.
7. Hold.
8. Repeat 5 times.

Photo 48 — *Lateral Stretch Sitting*

Lateral Stretch: Sitting

1. Sit facing forward, with your legs stretched out in front of you.
2. Cross your right leg over your left knee by bending your leg at the right knee and placing your right foot next to the outside of your straight left knee. *(Photo 48)*
3. Rotate your torso to the right, placing your left elbow outside your right knee.
4. Hold.
5. Repeat to the other side.
6. Hold.

***Variation:* This exercise may be varied by bending the straight leg as shown in *Photo 48.* Be sure both seat bones are touching the ground evenly, and that the shoulders remain level.

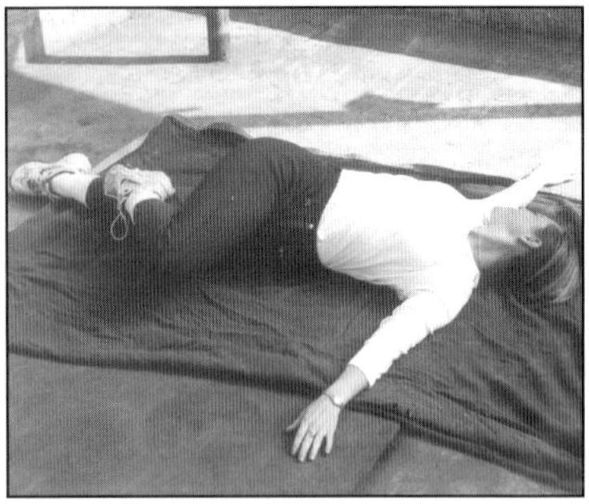

Photo 49 — *Lateral Stretch in Lying Position*

Lateral Stretch: Lying Down

1. Lie on your back, legs stretched out together in front of you, arms out to your sides at right angles to your body.
2. Bend your right knee and place your foot on the ground to the right of your left knee.
3. Press your right knee to the left, towards the ground. At the same time, turn your head to the right. *(Photo 49)*

**Keep your shoulders pressed down evenly into the ground.

4. Hold.
5. Repeat with the left knee bent, pressing the left knee to the right towards the ground.
6. Repeat 5 times.

Leg Stretches

Leg stretches are very valuable in improving coordination, range of motion, and suppleness. These factors help elongate the leg, which is so important for an elegant and effective position.

Forward Leg Stretch: Sitting

1. Sit on the ground with your legs stretched out to the sides.
2. Reach your arms up over your head while keeping your shoulders pressed down and your back as straight as possible. *(Photo 50A)*
3. Reach to the right, as far over toward your right leg as possible, while still facing forward. *(Photo 50B)*

** Keep both seat bones pressed evenly into the ground.

4. Hold.
5. Return to the forward position.
6. Reach over to the left, as far over the left leg as possible, while still facing forward.
7. Hold.
8. Return to the forward position.
9. Repeat 5 times.

Photo 50A — *Lateral Leg Stretch, Sitting Upright*

Photo 50B — *Lateral Leg Stretch to Right Facing Forward*

Lateral Leg Stretch: Sitting

1. Sit on the ground with your legs stretched out to the sides.
2. Reach your arms up over your head, while keeping your shoulders pressed down and your back as straight as possible.
3. Rotate your torso to the right, so you are facing your right leg.
4. Bend from the waist and reach your left arm down toward your right leg, as low as is comfortable. *(Photo 50C)*
5. Hold.

**Keep both seat bones pressed evenly into the ground.

6. Return to the forward position.
7. Repeat to the left side.
8. Hold.
9. Repeat 5 times.

Photo 50C — *Lateral Leg Stretch Rotating Torso Toward Leg*

Front Thigh Stretch

1. Stand in neutral.
2. Hold onto a stable support in front of you.
3. Lift your right foot behind you and grasp it with your right hand. *(Photo 51)*
4. Hold until you feel your thigh muscles relax.

**Keep your right thigh straight next to your standing left leg.

5. Repeat with the left leg.

Photo 51 — *Front Thigh Stretch*

Photo 52 — *Front Leg Stretch*

Photo 53 — *Front and Lateral Leg Stretch*

Photo 54 — *Back Leg Stretch*

Front Leg Stretch

1. Stand in neutral.
2. Bending your knee, raise your right foot and place it against something solid in front of you at approximately hip level.
3. Gently press your chest forward toward your foot. *(Photo 52)*
4. Hold.
5. Repeat 5 times.
6. Repeat with left leg, 5 times.

Front and Lateral Leg Stretch

1. Stand in neutral.
2. Lift your right leg forward in front of you onto something at waist level or above (the higher, the greater the stretch).

**Keep the hips facing front and even.

3. Reach forward over the leg. *(Photo 53, right side)*
4. Hold.
5. Repeat 5 times.
6. Repeat with the left leg, 5 times.
7. Repeat steps 1-6, lifting leg laterally for a lateral stretch. *(Photo 53, left side)*

Back Leg Stretches

1. Stand in neutral.
2. Hold onto something solid in front of you.
3. With your right hand, reach behind your back and grasp your right toe. Lift your right leg behind you, as far as is comfortable. *(Photo 54)*
4. Hold.
5. Repeat 5 times.
6. Repeat with your left leg, 5 times.

Hamstring Stretch From Step

1. Stand on the balls of your feet on a stool or step facing a counter, bar, or other solid support. *(Photo 55)*
2. Let your heels sink, feeling a gentle stretch in your hamstrings.

**You may place one foot on a higher step to ease the stretch.

3. Hold.
4. Repeat 5 times.
5. If you placed your feet at different levels, reverse your feet and repeat 5 times.

Photo 55 — *Ham String Stretch from Step*

Hamstring Stretch From Long Stride

1. Stand in front of something solid on which you can rest your arms.
2. Place one foot in front of the other, at least shoulder width apart, keeping your back leg straight. *(Photo 56, left side)*
3. Hold until you feel the gentle stretch in the hamstring. The back leg may be bent to further the stretch. *(Photo 56, right side)*

Photo 56 — *Ham String Stretch, Long Stride*

Leg Stretches: Forward Bend

1. Stand in neutral, with legs more than shoulder width apart, keeping your knees straight.
2. Bend forward from the waist and place your hands on your feet, while keeping your knees straight.
3. Hold. *(Photo 57, left side)*
4. Return to neutral.
5. Repeat 5 times.

***Variation:* In Step 1, bend your knees instead of keeping them straight and reach your arms horizontal to the ground and keep your back flat. *(Photo 57, right side)*

Photo 57 — *Leg Stretch Forward Bend with Legs Straight & Knees Bent*

Photo 58 — *Forward Leg Stretch, Sitting*

Forward Leg Stretches: Sitting

1. Sit with legs straight out in front of you.
2. Keeping your back straight, bend forward from the waist and grasp your toes or calves. *(Photo 58, left side)*
3. Hold.
4. Repeat 5 times.

***Variation:* In step 1, instead of straight legs, bend your knees and letting them fall apart, place the soles of your feet together. *(Photo 58, right side)*

Photo 59 —*Leg Stretch, Sitting,* Cross Legs

Leg Stretches: Sitting with Crossed Legs

1. Sit with legs straight out in front of you.
2. Cross your right leg over your left leg at the knee.
3. Placing your hands on your right leg, gently pull your body forward over your legs. *(Photo 59, left side)*
4. Hold.
5. Repeat 5 times.
6. Repeat with left leg, 5 times.

***Variation:* In step 1, bend and cross the right leg over the bent left leg and reach your arms forward to the ground. *(Photo 59, right side) Reverse leg and repeat stretch.*

8

Lungeing The Horse

> *"The ultimate goal . . . in this step in the horse's education . . . is the production of a happy horse that shall in due course under my saddle be as free and brilliant as nature can make him."*
>
> *– Henry Wynmalen*

Teaching your horse to lunge plays a valuable part in his training. In terms of the pyramid, it furthers the horse's development physically, mentally, emotionally, and spiritually. Physically, lungeing strengthens your horse's balance, suppleness and rhythm. Temporarily freed from the influence of the rider's weight and balance, the horse must support his own side of the wall, finding his natural balance. Thus it additionally helps in starting a young horse or exercising one that cannot be ridden. Mentally, the repetitious nature of lungeing and the reduction of outside stimuli increase the horse's focus on his work. Emotionally, lungeing creates a calmer, steadier attitude, as the horse learns to relax and stretch into the side reins. Spiritually, lungeing reinforces discipline. The horse quickly learns that by yielding to the pressures of the lunge line, side reins, lunge whip and shape, an immediate reward is evident. From the ground, you can observe your horse's progress in all four sides of the pyramid.

It is very important to use the correct tack, as this supports a successful training session. This includes a regular snaffle bit with a dropped or flash noseband, a lunge cavesson, a lunge line, lunge whip (long enough to touch the horse while on the circle), a saddle or surcingle, and side reins or lungeing draw reins.

The lunge line may be attached to the cavesson's middle ring for the mildest effect, since the mouth is not involved. An effective alternative is to run the lunge line through the inside ring of the snaffle bit and then pass it over the poll, or under the chin, and clip it to the opposite ring of the bit. Although these methods directly affect the mouth, they help balance the action of the bit because the line is connected to both sides of the bit. We don't advise connecting the lunge line solely to the inner ring because the bit is more easily pulled through the horse's mouth. Other methods of attaching the lunge line exist, which address specific problems. For specific correctional techniques, it is best to work with a knowledgeable trainer. Our purpose is to introduce the basic method.

If your horse has never been lunged, begin without the use of side reins. As he becomes confident in working in a circle shape around the handler, side reins may be introduced. Before you attach the side reins to the girth, make sure that the horse has learned to "give" to pressure. Horses that don't know this lesson may become frightened and back fiercely upon feeling the restraint of the side reins. Preparatory training is necessary to avoid this undesirable reaction.

The length of the side reins varies according to the degree of the horse's training. They should initially be attached quite long, so that the horse can barely find them, and low, close to the elbow. This encourages the horse to stretch his neck downward and forward. Gradually, over time, the side reins can be shortened and raised as the horse becomes better balanced and engaged. When a horse has trouble bending, you can shorten the inside side rein, at least one to two holes. Other techniques of attaching the reins between the front legs can be implemented. Consult with your trainer as to the pros and cons of this method concerning your horse.

Some horses fear a fixed contact with side reins. In such cases, sliding draw reins allow a variable contact, which may help such horses accept a contact with the bit. Other options include side reins with elastic or rubber donuts. Again, work with your trainer in implementing methods to address a specific problem.

Once your horse is tacked up appropriately for lungeing, several precautions will help to ensure a successful lungeing experience. Initially, lunge your horse in an enclosed area, such as a round pen, in order to prevent your horse from running out. An appropriate diameter consists of approximately a fifteen-meter circle. This size is small enough, so that you can touch your horse with the lunge whip, and large enough to avoid over stressing your horse's tendons, joints and muscles. Once your horse is obedient and dependable about lungeing, this enclosure is no longer necessary.

Before using a whip, check to make sure your horse accepts the use of the whip without reacting in fear. You may need to stroke the horse's body with the whip until he remains relaxed in the presence of the whip.

In the beginning, you might also wish to employ the aid of one or two assistants. *(Photo 60)* This helps teach the horse to move forward and stay on the circle shape. Initially, the handler holds the line at the center of the circle and the first assistant leads the horse at a walk on the circle shape. The second assistant holds the lunge whip, and stands to the left of the handler, when the horse travels to the right, and to the handler's right, when the horse travels to the left. This assistant must be alert and quick to respond by driving the horse forward upon the first indication of balking. It may be necessary to drive from behind, always keeping a safe distance. Once the horse understands the idea of moving forward in a circle, the first assistant is no longer necessary. When you can rely on consistent obedience from your horse, the second assistant can also be eliminated.

When lungeing your horse, your body, the horse's nose and hindquarters form the three points of a triangle. Position yourself in the middle of the circle and slightly behind the saddle, not in front of it, as this encourages the horse to turn in on you. Hold the line as if it is a rein, in the right hand for lungeing to the right and in the left hand for lunge-

Photo 60 — *Kandi, Serena, and Danielle assist in lungeing session.*

ing to the left. The rein hand also holds the surplus line, kept in open loops over the thumb, never encircling the thumb or the hand. *(Illustration S)* This allows you to feel the horse's mouth through the rein and to use your hand and arm in a similar manner as when you ride, making corrections or checking your horse more effectively into your back. By using one hand to handle the line, the other hand is free to control the whip and there is less chance of getting the line and whip tangled. As the horse moves around the circle, turn your body relative to his movement so that you are continually facing him, keeping your shoulders square as you rotate. Failure to rotate with your horse usually results in the horse's loss of attention to the work.

Carry the whip low, pointing towards the horse's hindquarters. Lift it to increase the horse's energy. If necessary, tap the horse on the haunches with the end of the whip. Avoid snapping the whip at the horse like a lion tamer, as often the horse becomes dull to the noise. If the horse collapses in on the shape, point the whip at his shoulder or create small ripples in the line, telling him to stay out.

Illustration S — *Trianglar placement of handler, horse, and lunge whip. Encircled diagram shows hand placement.*

Once your horse is comfortable with the circle shape, you may begin improving his actual training. The trot is most commonly schooled first, due to its natural repetitive beat. It is also usually better balanced than the canter. The first few minutes may be done in walk or trot without the side reins, or if the horse is comfortable with them, they may be attached long and low on the girth near the elbow.

A steady rhythm may be practiced and supported in all three gaits. The use of checks or tugs on the lunge line and a soothing voice will help slow down a rushed rhythm. You may need to encourage your horse to move out by clucking and pointing or tapping the whip at his hindquarters or raising the tone of your voice with your word command.

Transitions can also be practiced on the lunge line. Steady transitions from trot to canter and canter to trot can reinforce the horse's ability to maintain his balance, while smoothly executing these upward and downward changes. Properly adjusted side-reins will encourage the horse to stretch onto his top muscling. This assists in creating a strong back and hindquarters and a pretty arched neck. The continual bending of the circle shape strengthens and supples the inner hind leg and, through knowledgeable corrections, the horse can improve his balance into the outside rein. This training provides valuable preparation and support for riding the horse under saddle.

Most lungeing sessions can be concluded within approximately twenty minutes. Include travel in both directions in order to develop the horse evenly on both sides.

As a variation, lunge long-reining can prove useful with a young or disobedient horse. The dual reins allow greater control over speed and shape.

For a more advanced horse, long reining can aid in the development of half steps, piaffe and passage. However, lunge long-reining presents a greater challenge and requires more experience and knowledge to master. We recommend that you consult with an experienced trainer and/ or study some of the excellent videos demonstrating this technique.

Observing Your Horse's Progress

With correct lungeing, the horse's progress in balance, suppleness, rhythm, and eventual collection can be observed from the ground. For the purpose of illustration, we will describe three general levels of progress on the lunge line. In reality, progress occurs along a steady continuum. Not all horses may reach the third stage, but most horses can benefit greatly from lungeing.

Beginning Stage

In the beginning, the horse may appear stiff in the body with little or no ability to bend onto the circle shape. He may cut in or out on the shape to avoid the difficulty of bending. Due to a lack of balance and suppleness, the horse may also lean into the circle. The neck usually lacks top muscling or may even show greater bottom muscling, giving the appearance of a U-neck. *(Photo 61)* The stiffness in the horse's back frequently shows up as short strides in all gaits, as he fails to track up. Tracking up refers to the horse's ability to bring his hind feet into or beyond the prints left by the front feet, most easily visible in walk and trot.

At this stage, various forms of resistance often appear. The horse may fight by tossing his head or putting his tongue over the bit. He may become disobedient and pin his ears, charge or try to kick or strike the handler, rear or buck, back up or refuse to go forward, or attempt to change his direction.

Several explanations may account for the horse's resistance or disobedience. The horse may be too physically weak to carry himself for a normal lungeing session of approximately twenty minutes. In this case, a gradual lengthening of his flat work, interspersed with trail rides either under saddle or ponied, will help build up his stamina and muscling. Secondly, the horse may lack suppleness and balance, which can develop over time with correct lungeing. A third explanation may derive from a resistant or fearful attitude. This may be due to lack of training or previous mishandling. In this case, its useful to employ the aid of two assistants as previously mentioned. Finally, rule out various physical problems, such as leg or back injuries or discomfort, poorly fitting tack, mouth abscesses or teeth problems, or conformation difficulties.

At this stage, using long and low side reins allows the horse to reach and stretch into the bit. Initially, focus mainly on the trot. Then add trot to walk transitions. While lungeing with side reins, minimize walking on the lunge with young or green horses. Once your horse lunges at trot in a steady, balanced and calm manner, you can introduce short

Photo 61 — *Kimi demonstrates the beginning stage of lungeing.*

periods of canter, with transitions back to trot.

Repetition is helpful, yet it's important to sense when to stop. Look for a place to end while your horse is performing successfully, before he is over tired or bored. As with all training, reward even the smallest try by allowing the horse to walk, using verbal praise, changing the gait, or concluding the training session.

Intermediate

In the second stage, the horse demonstrates obedience to driving and checking aids and acceptance of the side reins. He stretches onto the top muscling and exhibits an accepting, quiet mouth by chewing softly or salivating. As he moves around the circle shape, he flexes at the poll and bends laterally, appropriate to the shape, while maintaining vertical body carriage. Finally, the transitions between the gaits become smooth and prompt. The horse demonstrates his increased confidence and balance by expressing his gaits with better rhythm and regularity. *(Photo 62)*

More Advanced

In the third stage, the horse demonstrates greater longitudinal and lateral suppleness. Longitudinal suppleness refers to an elastic connection from the hind legs over the back or "bridge" to the mouth and back again. The angles of the hind legs become more acute and they are carried more under the horse's body, thereby freeing the weight carried by the shoulders. The lateral suppleness refers to the horse elastically bending its whole body to the left and right without resistance. *(Photo 63)*

The side reins may be raised and shortened as a more collected balance is introduced. The horse accepts this shortened frame and performs the exercises and transitions between the gaits with accuracy, smoothness, rhythm and increased collection. He exhibits a well-developed, rounded top line and maintains connection with the bit and self-carriage consistently, while increasing and decreasing the size of the circle shape. When the horse is confident in his connection with the bit, he will chew it softly with his lips closed, never sucking back, gaping the

Photo 62 — *Tango demonstrates the intermediate stage.*

Photo 63 — *Konstellation demonstrates a more advance stage with raised side reins.*

mouth open, rolling the tongue around, or shaking and tossing the head. Self-carriage is obtained by the horse balancing himself more independently on his own legs without leaning onto the side reins or lunge line. In this stage you may increasingly ask for more collection from behind as you shorten and raise the side reins. Asking for more power from the hind legs enables the shoulders to find more freedom and lightness. Decreasing the size of the circle (to about 10 meters and then out again) for intermittent periods promotes strength, suppleness and balance.

Longitudinal suppleness increases as lengthens are integrated into the lungeing program. When lengthening the stride, the steps and frame of the horse will stretch out. The tempo, balance and alignment should not be sacrificed. Then when collecting back to the previous trot, the wheelbase is shortened but the activity of the hind legs is sustained. These transitions between the paces of the gaits, as well as transitions between the gaits, such as walk/canter and halt/trot improve obedience, balance, and collection.

If long reining is used, more advanced exercises such as lateral work, piaffe and passage may be incorporated. The Spanish Riding School is famous for implementing this type of training. Many books and videos are devoted to this classical art of long reining.

Lungeing The Rider: Mounted Exercises

9

“*At first the rider must learn to stay in the correct position whilst at the same time absorbing the movement of the horse . . . without losing his balance or needing to grip onto the horse.*”

– *Kyra Kyrklund*

Lungeing also enhances the rider's physical, mental, emotional and spiritual growth. Riding on the lungeline helps riders gain control over their body placement, carriage, rhythm and balance. Relieved of the necessity to control the horse's direction and speed, the focus may be concentrated on the rider. Inexperienced riders and more experienced riders with bad habits gain from this opportunity to focus on themselves, without worrying about the horse's direction or correctness. Performing exercises while being lunged allows the rider to establish an independent seat or to correct faulty habits. These exercises help the rider relax more fully, loosen various parts of the body and achieve better balance while performing isolated movements.

In terms of mental development, being lunged allows riders to focus more intently on their riding. Trusting the handler to control the horse, the rider can put full attention on gaining greater understanding of the position and the execution of aids. Experiencing thirty minutes of sustained focus, free from other distractions increases the rider's ability to maintain focus in other riding situations.

Being lunged also allows riders to grow emotionally. The increased security, created by the confines of the lunge arena and the support of the handler, allows riders to overcome fears and build courage and confidence.

Spiritually, being lunged promotes greater discipline; delaying gratification, accepting responsibility, dedicating oneself to truth, and balancing. When we submit to being lunged, we must delay the gratification of more fun or exciting riding experiences. Perhaps the greatest benefit comes from confronting the truth about our riding and accepting responsibility for our part. Since the handler controls the horse, we are freed from blaming the horse for our own problems. The handler's feedback allows us to see ourselves more truthfully and clearly. Being lunged develops better physical balance, but it also creates better balance in our training program by encouraging a flexible attitude towards learning. Many rigid beliefs about our horses or ourselves are loosened by being lunged.

Choose a horse that lunges reliably and a handler who is experienced and confident with lungeing. The horse should offer a steady, good rhythm and remain relaxed throughout the rider's movements. Some horses may become disturbed by the rider's movements during these exercises. Check to determine that your horse accepts these movements without reacting. If the horse becomes tense, the rider may become inhibited and fail to achieve the maximum benefit from these exercises. The handler should be able to control the horse, freeing the rider to focus on the exercises.

As with any exercises, you should follow several precautions. First, if you have any limitations due to injury or body structure, consult your physician or sports trainer, before attempting these exercises. Secondly, become familiar with each exercise before trying it. Use your coach's feedback to ensure that you are performing the exercises correctly, while maintaining proper body position. Third, listen to your body. Build up slowly over time to avoid muscle strain or injury and stop if you experience pain. Last of all, perform the movements slowly and quietly to avoid startling your horse.

While seated on the horse, begin each exercise from the correct mounted position described in *Chapter 6, The Rider's Position*. We will refer to this as the neutral position. At first, it may be difficult to maintain a correct, balanced position while performing the exercises. Whenever you or your coach notice that you've lost this position, correct yourself before continuing the exercise. With practice, you'll be able to stay relaxed and balanced, even while performing the most challenging exercises.

Begin by performing the exercises in the halt or walk. As your skill and confidence increase, you can try some of the following variations. You can increase the difficulty of each exercise by performing it in the trot or canter. When you're confident with an exercise, try closing your eyes briefly to increase the feeling of each movement. To emphasize the development of an independent seat, experiment with dropping the reins and/or stirrups.

The ground exercises, described in *Chapter 7, Stretch Toward Supple Riding,* for the neck, shoulders, arms, ribs and waist can be performed while mounted, with the exception of the Shoulder Press and the Arms Back Variation, bending forward. *(Photos 30B and 30C on page 53, and Photos 35, 36A, and 36B on page 55)*

Upper Body Stretches

Arms Out *(Photo 64A, Rotate in and out)*

1. Sit in neutral.
2. Stretch your arms out to your sides, shoulder level and parallel to the ground, with your palms facing upward.
3. Rotate from the waist towards the inside of the circle, as far as it is comfortable. *(Photo 64B)*
4. Hold 5 counts.
5. Return to center.
6. Repeat to the outside of the circle. (*Photo 64C*)
7. Hold 5 counts.
8. Return to center.
9. Repeat 5 times.

Photo 64A — *Lindsay demonstrates arms to side.*

Shoulders: Alternating Shoulders Presses

This exercise increases flexibility of the torso and awareness of the seat. If you hold tension in your torso and find bouncing a problem, this exercise will be especially beneficial. The alternating shoulder presses are performed in time with the horses stride in walk or trot to a count of five.

1. Sit in neutral.
2. Press your right shoulder down to the count of one.
3. Press your left shoulder down to the count of two.
4. Continue alternating shoulder presses for 5 counts.
5. Rest and focus on following your horses stride with your seat.
6. Repeat 5 times.

Photo 64B — *Rotate inwardly from the waist*

Arms: Reach and Touch

In addition to stretching the upper body, this exercise distracts a nervous rider, encouraging freedom of movement and therefore, relaxation. Children particularly enjoy this exercise. During this exercise, attempt to maintain correct seat and lower leg positions. You will achieve greater strength and body isolation if you do not use your opposite arm for support.

Photo 64C — *Rotate outwardly from the waist*

Photo 65A — *Krista demonstrates Arm Reaching Up.*

Photo 65B — *Bend From Waist and Reach Toward Horse's Ears*

Photo 65C — *Reach to Inside Toes*

1. Sit in neutral.
2. Raise your left arm high in the air, even with your ear, keeping your shoulders pressed down and level. *(Photo 65A)*
3. Bend forward from the waist and reach toward the horse's ears. *(Photo 65B)*
4. Return to neutral.
5. Raise your left arm high in the air as in step 2.
6. Reach down to touch your inside toe. (Photo 65C)
7. Return to neutral.
8. Raise your left arm up as in step 2.
9. Reach down across your body, trying to touch your right toe. *(Photo 65D)*
10. Return to neutral
11. Raise your left arm forward at shoulder height with your palm facing upward.
12. Rotate from the waist slowly towards your left, reaching towards the dock of your horse's tail. *(Photo 65E)*
13. Return to neutral.
14. Repeat with the other arm.
15. Repeat 5 times.

Leg Exercises:

Knees Up

This exercise will help you find your seatbones.

1 Sit in neutral.
2. Hold onto the pommel of the saddle to help steady your balance.
3. Bring both knees up as high as possible. *(Photo 66)* Let go of your hands to better test your balance.
4. Hold 5 seconds.
5. Allow your legs to stretch back down the saddle in the neutral position.
6. Repeat 5 times.

Photo 65D — *Reach to Outside Toes*

Photo 65E — *Reach to Tail*

Photo 66 — *Jana demonstrates Knees Up.*

Bicycling

This exercise will help loosen your thighs.

1. Sit in neutral.
2. Circle the right leg forward, using a bicycling motion.
3. Repeat 5 times.
4. Repeat 5 times with the left leg.
5. Allow legs to stretch back down the saddle in the neutral position.

Photo 67 — *Krista demonstrates Thigh Stretch.*

Thigh Stretch

If your legs tend to go forward into a chair position, the next two exercises will help you achieve a more stretched downward leg.

1. Sit in neutral
2. Bend your left leg at the knee, keeping your thigh vertical. *(Photo 67)*
3. Grasp your foot with your left hand.
4. Hold 5 seconds, allowing your thigh to relax.
5. Repeat with your right leg.
6. Repeat 5 times.
7. Allow legs to stretch back down the saddle in the neutral position.

Leg Swings

1. Sit in neutral.
2. With legs fairly straight, swing the right leg forward, as you swing the left leg backward.
3. Repeat 5 times.

Ankle Circles

This exercise helps loosen "frozen" ankles.

1. Sit in neutral.
2. Circle your ankles by pointing your toes up, in and then down.
3. Repeat 5 times.

**Since most riders error by turning their toes too far out, this exercise helps the rider correct this fault by turning the toes in. If you tend to toe in while riding, you can alter this exercise by pointing your toes up, out and then down in a continual circle.

Developing The Seat

An effective seat is one of the most valuable assets to effective riding. Practicing the three basic seats, while being lunged, will help you to differentiate between them and the transitions created by their effective use. Chapter 11 "Understanding and Improving the Gaits," provides greater detail regarding the effective use of the seats.

The Driving Seat

The driving seat is used to create more energy. Upward transitions, mediums, extensions, passage and half halts utilize the driving seat. To accomplish this seat, stretch your upper body upwards, push your seatbones down into the pommel of the saddle, close your lower legs, and tighten your lower back and abdomen.

The Following Seat

The following seat maintains a certain gait or pace. It helps the horse find or steady the rhythm of the walk, trot, or canter. This seat varies, depending on the horse's gait. In the walk, the rider's hips and hands move in opposition to one another on a horizontal plane, following the motion of the horse. In the sitting trot, the rider's seat and hips follow the movement of the horse's body, while the hands remain still. In the canter, the rider's hips and hands follow the horse's motion in unison, on a horizontal plane.

The Stilling Seat

The stilling seat is used for downward transitions, slowing down the tempo, and for half halting the horse for more sitting with the hind legs. To perform the stilling seat, stretch your upper body tall, think of stilling or quieting your seat as the horse is moving and brace the muscles of the lower back. As a photograph stills action, a stilling seat creates a slowing of your horse's action.

Exercises For Developing The Effect of The Seat

It is both humbling and enlightening to realize how clearly the horse can respond with little or no use of the hand aids. Working these exercises on the lunge, without using the reins, will help you focus solely on your seat and allow you to experience the power of this aid. The long-term benefit of this will discourage overuse of the hand aids thereby saving your horse's mouth.

Halting from the Seat

Help your horse find the halt by quieting your seat only. Use the stilling seat, making sure your seatbones are down in the saddle. You may close your knees to assist the halt ONLY IF your seatbones are already down in the saddle. If you pinch your knees and thighs without your seatbones being down, the horse will probably not halt. In fact, the use of knees and thighs alone often causes the horse to jig or quicken its pace.

Your horse may not respond initially. In this case, go back to the following seat and reattempt the stilling seat. It may be necessary to close your fists the first few times to bring the horse's attention to your seat. Reward your horse generously when you get the desired result.

Transitions Between the Gaits

While on the lunge, use your seat, without using your hands, to make transitions from one gait or pace to another. As soon as the horse performs the desired result, immediately adjust your seat to the new gait being performed. This exercise will help you perfect the clarity of the aids given by your seat, back and legs.

Walk to Trot and Trot to Walk

1. Establish the walk with the following seat.
2. Stretch your body tall and apply the driving seat , as you think of developing the trot.
3. Use your following seat in the sitting trot, focusing on the rhythm, your body alignment, and sitting tall and quiet.
4. Stretch up again and apply the stilling seat, as you think of developing the walk. As your horse walks, return to the following seat in the rhythm of walk.
5. Repeat this sequence, until you achieve predictable results.

   This exercise can be applied to all transitions between the gaits.

Transitions Within the Gaits

While on the lunge, you can clarify the effective use of your seat to develop the paces within the gaits by alternating between the driving, following and stilling seats.

This exercise can be applied to developing lengthens, collection, and medium paces. Due to the size of the circle, we do not advise concentrated work on extensions as this may result in injury to your horse.

Working Trot to Lengthening the Stride and Back

1. Establish a rhythmic working trot and maintain with a following seat.
2. Stretch your body tall and while keeping the rhythm of trot, apply the driving seat.
3. As your horse lengthens the stride, maintain the following seat, posting or sitting.
4. Stretch your body tall and apply a combination of the stilling and following seats to return to the working trot. Too strong of a stilling seat may result in a downward transition to walk.

This exercise can be used within all three of the gaits. You should strive to maintain rhythm and correct use of the horse's top muscling as you repeat these transitions within the paces of the gaits. Through repetition and clarity of your aids, you will teach your horse to be predictable, generous, and calm.

10

The Aids

"Horses are extremely sensitive to our body movements and will respond to both correct and incorrect aids."

– Betsy Steiner

The horse and rider are connected like the outer and inner walls of the pyramid. The inner wall, the rider, influences the outer wall, the horse, through the aids.

The aids provide a non-verbal, physical means to communicate with our horse. They work in harmony together, much like the many instruments in a symphony. The orchestra is made up of brass, strings, winds, and percussion. The aids consist of natural aids; the legs, hands, seat, back, and weight, and artificial aids; the voice, whip, and spurs. Each instrument may play different notes, just as the hand, seat or legs may operate differently. Yet the different parts contribute to a harmonious, whole composition. *(Illustration T)*

The means to create a symphony are controlled by the principles of musical composition. When these principals are followed, the end result, such as Vivaldi's *Four Seasons*, is a pleasure to experience. However, when the principles are ignored and the newly formed teenage garage band jams late into the night, the "music" becomes a disturbance of the peace. In a similar manner, the underlying principles of the aids provide a disciplined means to achieve the desired end: the light, harmonious dressage movements performed in unity by horse and rider.

We've identified eight principles that will help you understand and apply the aids correctly. There may be other principles, but we feel that even though the words may vary, our eight principles take into account the intent behind other terms. Our eight principles include giving aids that are **accurate, continual, consistent, immediate, appropriate in intensity, fair, preparatory** and **dynamic**.

Illustration T — *The Aids work in harmony like a Symphony.*

Accurate aids must be applied from a correct position. They are an addition to good riding that is being offered the horse, not in place of it. In other words, effective overall riding should not cease when the aids are applied. This idea may seem obvious, but it is often a difficult concept to act upon. For example, when Becky was learning the leg aids for canter, she would invariably fall in front of the vertical as her outside leg came back. Then her horse would lurch off on the forehand and buck in response to becoming so imbalanced. When Becky learned to maintain her correct body alignment and deep seat while asking with her canter aids, her horse picked up a well-balanced canter.

It's easy to be so concerned with giving a particular aid that the rest of our body falls apart. If the various musical sections of the orchestra suddenly played different melodies, the listener would probably react in confusion or disbelief. This analogy applies to our horse, who becomes confused by contradictory aids and may react by becoming tense or acting out. In the case of the symphony, the conductor must stop the orchestra and refocus all the performers on a common measure. Frequently riders respond to their horse's confusion with punishment. After repeated interactions like this, horses often get sullen, tight, short-fused, or negative. As riders, we can take a cue from the conductor by stopping, correcting our position and focusing on the accurate, harmonious application of all our aids.

Illustration U — *Focus in clearly on your intentions when applying the aids.*

Developing accurate aids can be approached from both the left brain in a cognitive manner and the right brain in an intuitive manner. Many books detail the accurate placement of aids, the "how to" for each movement. Understanding the aids intellectually and committing them to memory will help you in applying them. However, the "how" must be built on the foundation of "what" you want. A clear picture of what you want to achieve and what this looks and feels like is paramount. Watching other good riders perform both live and on video speaks directly to the right brain by encoding a visual image of what the aids seek to create.

The Aachen Composite offers a right-brained approach to the FEI movements and tests. In this video, international top riders like Monica Theodorescu, Nadine Cappellman-Biffar and Anky von Grunsven perform Prix St. George, Intermediare I, Intermediare II, and Grand Prix tests. Choose a rider that seems to speak to you and imagine yourself as this rider. Become so familiar with the images that you can see them in your mind without the aid of the video. In the introduction to this video, Robert Dover reminds us that it is our responsibility to convey what we want to our horse. He stresses that thinking is a powerful aid when it serves a "crystal clear" intention. If what you want is fuzzy, even though you understand how to apply the aids, you will be unable to create a clear, concise result. (*Illustration U*)

Another method of using the right brain is to take advantage of riding a school master horse. This will allow you to experience how "what" you want feels. Often the light goes on after feeling what a balanced canter, an extension or a half pass is all about.

Continual aids keep the communication with our horse constant. The following story told by Dennis Benpo Merzel, an American Zen teacher illustrates this principle. He tells of being invited into the cockpit of a 747 bound for Hawaii. There he watched a computer called Fred serve as the navigator. Each time the 747 goes a little off course, Fred computes a correction and immediately relays it to George, the computer who steers the plane. So Fred communicates the correction and George responds by adjusting the plane's direction. Amazing as it may seem, the plane is "off course" almost 90% of the time. This means that every few seconds Fred directs George. Sound like riding? The fact that as dressage riders we're navigators, not passengers, seems pretty obvious. Yet, how many times do we forget to follow up on an aid, expecting our horse to stay on course?

This story helped Margie realize that the aids are continual and that this constant interaction between herself and her horse was a fundamental principle of the aids. "Once I understood this, I could be more like Fred. I stopped expecting one or two applications of an aid to get us around the circle. This allowed me to want to keep the conversation going between me and my horse," she explained. We hope this story will help you embrace the principle of continual aids.

Consistent aids reinforce our horse's obedience. When a horse knows that sometimes he's expected to perform a certain way, but sometimes he isn't, he will be erratic in his performance. This principle applies both on the ground and under saddle. Aaron, a cowboy and horse trainer, worked with Chuck on this principle. Chuck complained that Blazer crowded into his space. "Well now," Aaron mused with a slow grin, "I wonder who taught him that." Sometimes Chuck backed Blazer off when he came too close, but other times he patted him on the head and allowed him to nuzzle his chest. How Chuck responded depended on Chuck's mood and what he wanted to accomplish with Blazer. For Blazer, it seemed that crowding was okay. In a similar fashion, Erin sometimes allowed Glory to walk off while she was mounting and on other occasions required him to stand. Glory interpreted this, as "It's okay to peel off!" When Erin consistently required Glory to stand, he stopped moving off before she was ready. When we take responsibility to correct our own inconsistent methods, our horse's behavior often improves.

Immediate aids refer to the effective timing of both corrections and rewards. To be most effective, the correction or reward must be applied within three seconds of our horse's behavior. Often riders wait too long to apply an aid. (*Illustration V*) When Jennifer was first learning to keep Sheba on the bit, she typically waited for Sheba to come above the bit before applying the necessary combination of aids to keep her horse round and on the bit. By improving the immediacy of her timing, Jennifer was able to teach Sheba to remain on the bit.

This same principle applies to rewarding the horse. Rewards given through the voice, a pat with the hand, or a lightening of the pressure of the leg, seat, or hand aids reinforce whatever behavior your

Illustration V — *You've got three seconds!*

horse is performing at that moment. Barbi encourages her riders to reward the slightest try the horse offers. Kathy learned this principle when she asked Jessie to flex to the left, but then was late in rewarding the moment Jessie yielded to the flexion. By the time Kathy rewarded Jessie with a giving rein, Jessie had already become heavier and tense. If we look at Kathy's timing, we realize that she was rewarding the heavy, tense response rather than the left flexion.

Aids that are **appropriate in intensity** ensure our horse's attention, respect, and obedience. Sometimes we may whisper our message and sometimes we must shout it. Barbi tries to use as little aid as she has to, but as much aid as she needs to in order to train toward the desired result. Most of us have had the experience of closing our leg to ask for a forward response and our horse half-heartedly responds. Then we develop the ineffective habit of nagging with our legs, saying "move, move, move" with each stride. This sounds a little bit like telling our kids its time for bed and we suddenly become angry when a half hour passes and they're still in front of the television set. Our problem here is one of intensity.

In teaching your horse to move forward to a lightly applied lower leg, you can apply this principle. Begin by stretching your upper body, pushing your seatbones down and forward, and closing your lower legs into the horse's sides. If no forward response or a lazy forward response occurs, instantly kick the horse sharply on his sides, repeatedly if necessary, until the horse produces the desired forward movement. When a quiet aid is applied and ignored, it must be followed by an immediate wake-up call. Then reward the horse's quick response by a cessation of the staccato correction and a soothing voice or the touch of your hand on his neck. Retest the quiet aid to see if the horse remembers to listen attentively. Repeat your intense correction as necessary until the horse produces the immediate forward response to the quiet leg aid. This same principle of appropriate intensity applies to the other aids as well.

Fair aids are aids that the horse has a reasonable chance to understand and execute. We feel that aids are unfair when the seven other principles of aids are ignored. Fair aids are accurate, continual, consistent, immediate, appropriate in intensity, preparatory and dynamic. Such aids give the horse the best chance to produce the desired result.

Waldemar Seunig, Austrian rider, judge, and author, stresses that fairness also resides in the rider's attitude towards the horse. He states that, "The horse has been able to judge the rider's good nature by the fact that he was on the lookout, so to speak, for the slightest indication of responsiveness to his controls to reward the horse, and that he was magnanimous in forgetting to punish when the mistake was due to clumsiness or inadequate understanding." Being quick and generous with our praise and tolerant of our horse's honest mistakes supports fairness.

Fair aids are taught progressively. Many children have been traumatized by the old adage of "sink or swim", when well meaning adults threw them into the lake. In teaching our horse a new system of communication, it is helpful to introduce one aid at a time in a progressive manner.

The following exercise illustrates a progressive lesson to teach lateral flexion. While standing next to your horse's head, apply a firm, gentle pressure to the left rein. *(Photo 68A, see page 83)* The horse should yield to the pressure with a slight lateral flexion in the poll area. You may need to stroke his neck with the other hand or speak softly, so that he does not become fearful. The moment the horse responds with a gesture of yielding, you must immediately release your pressure on the rein. It may take a few moments for the horse to find that yielding to the pressure will result in a release of the pressure by his handler. Repeat this exercise, praising each correct response. Once your horse understands left lateral flexion from pressure on the left, repeat this process on the right side. *(Photo 68B)* Next, the same exercise may be repeated while under saddle. *(Photos 68C, 68D)* After simple lateral flexion at the poll is understood, the leg and seat may be added with the flexing aids to achieve clearer throughness and on-the-bitness at the halt, walk, trot, canter and so on.

Preparatory aids prepare the horse to successfully produce our desired results. The half-halt is the method used to help bring the horse to an improved state of balance and attention. It is applied by using the driving aids by the leg and seat to the suppling

Photo 68A — *Left Flexion Unmounted*

Photo 68B — *Right Flexion Unmounted*

Photo 68C — *Left Flexion Mounted*

Photo 68D — *Right Flexion Mounted*

yet somewhat restraining hand, followed by a moment of light. It is used repeatedly before, during and after all the work performed.

Several interacting factors influence the degree of preparation needed: the horse's level of dressage training, his responsiveness, his emotional state and various environmental factors. In general, the more educated a horse, the less advance preparation he will need to respond to our aids. When Kathy purchased her new seventeen hand, untrained sluggish Dutch Warmblood, she was surprised at the degree of advance preparation her horse needed to halt, to move off the leg, to turn or to maintain a circle shape. She had been accustomed to the quick response of her previous mount, a trained Thoroughbred! Likewise, a more responsive horse will execute the aids more readily with less preparation. A horse's emotional state also influences the amount of preparation needed. An emotionally charged, reactive horse often needs greater preparation than a calm, steady horse. Finally, challenges presented by the environment such as frightening obstacles, poor footing, threatening weather, or lack of defined boundaries can all increase the necessary preparation time. For example, strong leg yield aids, with repeated half-halts, may need to be applied well in advance of a new or threatening object in order to keep the horse on the rail.

Dynamic aids refer to the changeable, flowing quality of the aids. An orchestra produces a live performance in which the relationships among its various parts continually change. The bass section provides a steady back up beat, then can surprise with a sudden explosion. The strings may harmonize together to carry the melody, or a violinist may play an intricate virtuoso solo. This is also true of the riding aids for as horse and rider, we give a continual live performance. From moment to moment we must adjust the mix of the previous seven principles of our aids in order to achieve a harmonious ride. What worked the previous moment must be adjusted in the present moment. This means that at times, we must emphasize one or more or the previous seven principles while maintaining the others, in order to achieve our results.

Let's take a closer look at how dynamic aids operate in a lengthen across the diagonal. Initially, you may be preparing to perform a lengthen when you realize that your horse has become dull to the driving aids. In this moment **intensity** must be stressed, in order to wake up your horse so that he responds with sufficient impulsion to produce a lovely lengthening. Next, you sustain the **accurate** and **continual** nature of your aids to carry the lengthen to the end marker. Applying the principle of **preparation**, you notice a wet spot at X and prepare in your half-halt by maintaining a steady rhythm with your seat and a firmer supportive framework with your leg and rein aids. Finally, your horse produces the best lengthen he is currently capable of, yet less than you know he will develop over time. You wish it had been better to impress a spectator. However, applying the principle of **fair** aids, you reward his performance by not pushing for more, stroking his neck at completion and then moving on to another lesson. The total picture of our successfully performed lengthen across the diagonal is **dynamic**, a live performance that continually changes according to whatever is needed in the moment to create a harmonious performance.

We feel that when these eight principles of **accurate, continual, consistent, immediate, appropriate in intensity, fair, preparatory and dynamic aids** are employed, the end product will be a confident, happy team that displays the harmony and joy of dressage. These eight principles are the means to achieving this end. Reiner Klimke states, "The schooling in obedience to the rider's aids should be carried out with such sensitivity that the horse's happiness in his work is evident. This joy should carry over to the spectators; they should experience how an independently moving horse is presented by a rider using almost invisible aids."

11

Understanding and Improving The Gaits

"The rules of the FEI dictate that in dressage competition only the horse's natural movements – primarily the three basic gaits: walk, trot, and canter – should be given greater expression and lightness. . . . The philosophy behind this is clear: we want to develop the horse's natural movements from the three basic gaits –[walk, trot, and canter] – and leave it at that."

– Reiner Klimke

Dressage strives to develop big, fluid, expressive gaits. In this chapter, we will focus primarily on the horse's physical development. However, keep in mind that all sides of the pyramid are connected and influence each other. Therefore, we will at times refer to the mental, emotional or spiritual aspects of developing the gaits. More often than not, we must develop an improved gait over what the horse initially offers us. The walk should maintain an even four beat rhythm, the trot a steady two beat rhythm, and the canter an equal three beat rhythm followed by a moment of suspension. The walk, trot, and canter can all be improved in terms of regularity, relaxation, purity, and expression.

When working on improving the gaits, the rider must maintain a steady, relaxed and correct position, while utilizing an effective application of the aids. Both the rider's position and effective use of the aids form the base for achieving on-the-bitness, throughness, connection, rhythm, balance, softness and freedom from resistance. These qualities are essential to expressive gaits.

The importance of properly fitting tack cannot be overly emphasized. A saddle that constricts shoulder movement or is too close on the nuchal ligament adjacent to the spine, can not only restrict free articulation of the horses' joints and swinging back, but it can even cause lameness. Poor fitting bridles and bits can prevent elastic connection and a soft acceptance of the bit. Barbi has had the fortunate opportunity of working with Schleese Saddlery for very positive results in improving the horses' gaits. After measuring both the horse and rider, they create custom saddles that maximize optimum movement.

The rider provides a correct position and the effective use of aids. The horse contributes the willingness to move forward in the desired direction. As you perform the following exercises, this base of correct position and effective aids must be preserved at all times. Occasionally, you may need to back up and attend to the quality of your base, before moving ahead with the quantity. The concept of forward provides the bottom line to remember throughout the training process. Without the horse's willingness to move forward in the desired direction in response to the aids, RETURN to GO and DO NOT COLLECT $200! *(Illustration W)*

Developing the Walk

The walk is a marching pace in which the horse's feet follow one another in a four beat footfall. It should maintain four even, regular beats. The footfalls should be evenly spaced between the left hind, left fore, right hind, and right fore. Adequate freedom of the joints should permit at least some overstep of the hind feet stepping in front of the prints of the fore feet. The hind feet and fore feet should align on two tracks, indicating straightness in the horse's way of going. Ideally the height of the steps should be the same. Finally, the horse must be relaxed in both mind and body, offering full use of his back in order to maximize the chance of improving any weakness in the walk. The *USA Equestrian Rule Book* defines the five types of walk as free, working, collected, medium, and extended. We suggest that you refer to the *USA Equestrian Rule Book* for definitions of these five paces of the walk.

Since the walk is not an exciting gait, riders often neglect to work on it, only to be surprised when they receive low marks in competition. On the other hand, riders often work the walk incorrectly, prematurely attempting collection, and consequently damage the gait. The walk must be approached tactfully with knowledge and good timing to improve its quality. Whereas the trot and canter can be greatly improved through lungeing, the walk is best enhanced off the lunge. The following approaches and exercises can be implemented to improve all phases of the walk.

The biggest obstacles to achieving a relaxing, marching walk come from several rider faults. As discussed previously, the rider's hands must follow opposite the rider's hips to support the mechanics of the walk. Frozen hands restrict the natural forward and back movement of the horse's head and neck.

Illustration W – *No Forward . . . No Game!*

Gripping the legs, freezing the seat, and pushing the feet against the stirrups cause the horse to tense his back, inhibiting a relaxed, reaching stride. For a quick fix, drop your stirrups, open your knees and settle into your seatbones. This simple exercise often improves the walk immediately.

The horse's mind-set either contributes or detracts from developing a good walk. By using good timing in both the arena and on the trail, the rider can enhance the horse's chance for success. Since relaxation is essential in developing the walk, avoid presenting this work when the horse is anxious. Factors, such as feeding times, new environments, separations from buddies or foals, and unusual outside distractions may greatly interfere with the horse's ability to relax and concentrate. At times the horse may be too anxious or fresh to obediently maintain clear, marching walk steps. In this case, schooling the trot or canter first allows the horse to discharge excess energy and mentally focus on his work. After a good warm-up in these gaits, the horse will often welcome the walk as a time for rest and relaxation.

Trail riding provides an excellent opportunity to

work on the walk. The horse usually welcomes being out in nature and experiencing a change in pace from arena work. Balance and coordination naturally improve as the horse maneuvers around natural obstacles. This changed setting offers a new approach to slowing down, being responsive, and walking obediently.

The following strategies can promote successfully training the walk while trail riding. Putting a jigging horse in the lead, walking in pairs, leg yielding, and trotting to keep up with the group, enhance the horse's inclination to walk. As a more extreme correction, walking or leg yielding in a small circle helps dissipate tension by loosening the horse's back and making the hind legs cross under his body. These techniques may prove handy on returning home, when horses often attempt to jig or hurry rather than walk steadily. The "yo-yo" exercise involves leaving and returning home repeatedly, until the horse looses the desire to hurry home. In each set, the rider must remain calm and use one or more of the previously discussed relaxation techniques to obtain a good walk. In order to improve your horse's walk, select riding companions who respect trail manners. This involves awareness of maintaining good distance, remaining with the group, keeping a steady pace, and practicing trail safety.

The use of ground poles encourages the horse to stretch into longer strides in the walk. When correctly spaced for each individual horse's stride, they can also assist in steadying the rhythm of the gait. By experiencing the correct 1-2-3-4 sequences of good walk steps, both the horse and rider can learn how it should feel. This feel can then be repeated around the arena. Dr. Reiner Klimke's book, *Cavalletti,* provides an excellent resource for the rider, who wishes to incorporate ground poles in the training program.

Another effective exercise in developing a horse's walk is to practice having the horse let you change him in the walk. Here the emphasis is on the word let. Only through the horse's trusting, willing attitude of letting himself be changed in the walk, will he maintain the relaxation so essential to a good walk. Yet, this is a difficult concept to teach. We can convey the practical aids to change the walk, but the sensitivity to open the horse's willingness to let himself be changed must be sought after and intuitively sensed by the rider. The rider's patience and calmness facilitate the horse's ability to relax, which is essential for a good walk.

How we ride the walk can lengthen the frame and stride or shorten the frame and stride. To ask for a longer frame and stride, stretch your upper body taller letting your seat feel heavy, and relax down in the saddle. Let your seat generously follow the increased striding offered by the horse as you apply your leg aids. Your left leg nudges gently against the horse's side as he carries weight over his right foreleg. Alternately, your right leg nudges gently against the horse's side as he carries weight over his left foreleg. Using the leg aids in this timely fashion signals the horse's alternate hind leg to come further under his body in a larger step. By increasing your leg command, following with your hips, and following with your hands opposite your hips, you allow the horse to respond with a more generous stride.

As the horse stretches more down and forward into the walk, allow the rein contact to stretch more down and forward as well. This is how to practice "free walk on a long, stretched rein." Maintain the 1-2-3-4 rhythm and a definite march while lengthening the stride. The rhythm maintained by your seat and the stretch in the rein contact allow for this desired result. Always be careful not to rush the correct rhythm needed by each horse to establish a correct walk, as this can cause lateral steps. When ridden correctly, you should feel the horse's back lift, become more relaxed, and act as a bridge connecting the hind legs through the reins to the bit. The rider's aids should barely be visible with no obvious banging of the legs against the horse's sides or surging forward and backwards out of the correctly held leg position. The success of this exercise, as with all others, demands that the horse must be responsive to the driving, restraining, bending and suppling aids, discussed in *Chapter 10, The Aids.*

To ask for a shorter frame and stride, stretch your upper body and melt into your seat bones. Your legs continue their soft, alternating nudges. To facilitate a softer transition from long to shorter reins, shorten the inside rein first, and then the outside rein. You may also use the corners or a circle shape encouraging lateral flexion for a similar result. Your seat may assist in tactfully pushing the horse forward into the following hands while keeping the walk rhythm steady.

In addition to the previous suggestions and exercises, practicing lateral dressage movements such as many variations of leg yields, shoulder-in, haunches-in, renvers, and half pass, plus changes in the figures and patterns improve the quality of the walk. One of the main faults to a correct walk is that the horse takes on lateral, pace-like steps. This may be the result of conformational weakness, tension in the back, premature, or incorrect collection. The use of leg yielding and counter leg yielding provide an especially effective correction for lateral walks. In general, lateral exercises help the horse be more accepting and pliable, and thus enhance the walk, making the horse a greater pleasure to ride. A detailed discussion of these exercises is beyond the scope of this book. We suggest that you refer to books, video tapes, and your trainer in order to build your expertise in lateral work.

Developing the Trot

The trot is a two beat gait performed in two tracks in which the horse's legs hit the ground in diagonal pairs, separated by a moment of suspension. The left hind and right fore form one pair and the right hind and left fore form the other pair. The 1-2 rhythm must maintain an even tempo, neither speeding up nor slowing down. The trot should be free, active, regular, and balanced. In a free and active trot, the horse's shoulders and hindquarters articulate freely, allowing the hind feet to step energetically into or in front of the prints of the fore feet. The collected trot permits a shorter step while maintaining increased activity. The steps should be even in reference to length of stride and level in terms of vertical height. The horse should maintain straightness in the alignment of its body according to the direction of travel. Finally, the horse maintains balance by carrying his weight evenly in terms of right and left, and sufficiently on his haunches to perform the required task. In addition to these qualities, a good trot possesses suppleness and elasticity, which depend upon a pliable, swinging back. Relaxation and focus aid the horse to maximize his potential. The *USA Equestrian Rule Book* defines four types of trot: working, collected, medium, and extended. We suggest that you refer to the *USA Equestrian Rule Book* for definitions.

Lungeing can serve as a useful tool in developing the trot. It allows the horse to work on his own balance, without the additional weight of the rider. Even when the rider sits in a balanced, correct position, the additional weight alters the horse's natural balance. This is compounded when the rider's position is distorted and/or if the aids are inappropriately applied. For best results set up the work session in a quiet setting with good footing. Have the appropriate tack fitted to your horse and have assistants available if you expect to need them, as described in *Chapter 8: Lungeing The Horse.*

As with the walk, once the rider can follow the horse's movement in the trot with an elegant, correct posture and supple joints, the horse will have an easier time to improve the trot. As we've mentioned before, the rider's balance greatly affects the horse's balance. The rider's rhythm also influences the rhythm taken on by the horse. If the rider posts or sits to a steady cadenced rhythm, the horse will tend to follow that rhythm. This is easier said than done, especially when negotiating corners, figures, transitions and developing lengthens. This challenge is magnified when dealing with green or resistant horses, unexpected environmental stimuli and changes in footing. The following suggestions can assist the establishment of a steadier rhythm and an appropriate tempo.

1. *Count the rhythm out loud.* First count the rhythm that the horse is offering. This helps you become conscious of the rhythm, which precedes any attempt to improve it. You might notice that the horse's rhythm is unsteady or the tempo is too fast or too slow. Next, emphasize the steadiness and the tempo of your count and move your body, either rising or sitting, to that beat. This may entail getting feedback from a knowledgeable trainer or experienced helper, who can assess the best tempo for your horse at his stage of training.

2. *Wear a metronome to reinforce the rhythm.* Be sure your horse is desensitized to the sound before using this method while riding! Set the metronome to an appropriate tempo for your horse's gait.

3. *Ride to music.* With a little time and effort, you can select music appropriate to your horse's gait with the aid of a metronome. At the very least, listening to various musical pieces expands your awareness of rhythm. *(Illustration X)*

4. *Ride with a partner.* Select a partner who competently maintains a steady pace. This may be helpful in schooling a young or green horse. Always be careful to maintain a safe distance between horses to avoid being kicked.

In addition to maintaining a correct position, the rider's body can be used to enhance the quality of the trot. In the rising trot, the manner in which the rider posts can either flatten or expand the quality of the trot. For example, some riders post low to the saddle in a horizontal, rubbing fashion. The horse, in response, takes on a flat, low to the ground stride. When riders maintain a free moving post, balanced over their legs, with even and sufficient lift, the horse is free to swing and lift his back during the moment of suspension. In the sitting phase, the rider's seat should meet the horse's back softly to discourage hollowing or tensing of his back muscles. This is especially true in the sitting trot, where the seat and lower back must swing in harmony with the horse's movement.

Correct hand placement, an elastic contact, and effective hand aids assist the development of the trot. In review, remember that in general the proper hand placement involves carrying the hands evenly, and aligned from the elbow through the hand to the bit. Unlike the walk and canter, the horse's head

Illustration X —
As with dancing, keeping the beat is very important.

and neck remain relatively still while trotting. An elastic contact from the rider's hand to the horse's mouth means that the hands follow any small or unexpected movement of the horse's head to prevent inappropriately bumping the horse's mouth. In the rising trot, an elastic contact means that the elbow joints open and close slightly in order to maintain a steady, even hand position. In sitting trot, the hands hold a steady quiet place, never becoming rigid or bouncing up and down. When the horse trusts the rider's hands and contact with his mouth, he will more confidently stretch down and forward into the contact. This coupled with better use of his back and hindquarters allows him to be ridden more effectively on the bit.

The hand aids can refer to flexing the wrist, pressing the thumbs down, sponging the fingers, forming and releasing the fist, or lightening the contact for a moment of giving. Supported by the leg, seat, back and weight, the hand aids can attempt to help supple the horse's stiffness, tension, or resistance held both in his body, jaw and the atlas/axis joint (the point where the head and neck meet).

When the horse yields confidently through the atlas/axis joint, he more willingly allows himself to be changed by the rider. This is the precursor to developing the correct positioning and overall bending. A valuable exercise consists of flexing the horse slightly to the right or left at the atlas/axis joint, without altering the direction of travel or the alignment of the body. The rider quietly sustains a flexed position of the wrist, until the horse yields his head position. At this moment, the rider immediately relaxes the wrist. The timing regarding the moment of giving is essential. This exercise relaxes the horse's mind and body and thereby can enhance the quality of the trot. Great positive changes can be achieved through tactful training in this area. Refer to the exercise on page 83, Photos 68A through 68D.

In the trot, the leg aids may be used in either a quiet, sustaining manner or an abrupt, correcting technique. Care must be taken to maintain correct upper body and hand position, since frequently, using the legs may compromise the rider's position. The legs aids can help develop the trot, achieve straightness or create bending. To enhance the trot, the legs are used in time with the gait. In the posting trot, the lower leg must hold its correct position and gently squeeze the horse's sides during the sitting phase. In the sitting trot, the lower leg gently closes the horse's side each beat of the trot. By applying a quiet, rhythmic leg aid, the rider maintains rhythm, engagement and impulsion (compression and thrust of the hind legs). To correct a lethargic trot, use the approach described in *Chapter 10 The Aids,* regarding the appropriate intensity of aid application. As always, the aids should be as little as you need and as much as you require in order to create the desired results.

Anytime there is a change in direction, pattern, pace or gait, the footing, or the environment, the rider must prepare the horse to remain stable. By perceiving and assessing such variables, the rider can implement appropriate supportive aids. This involves remembering to maintain the rhythm of the seat and the correct, effective use of the aids and half-halts to ensure the horse's proper bend, balance connection and on-the-bitness. The degree of preparation varies according to each horse's temperament and training. This attentive riding allows for properly bent corners, consistent shapes, straight lines and steady rhythm. This in turn will ensure better self-carriage, balance, use of the hind legs, and a more relaxed mind.

Trail riding is very beneficial in enhancing the trot. In addition to refreshing the horse's mind and attitude, trail riding can improve rhythm, strength, balance, impulsion and obedience. These qualities can be improved by working the horse on gradually sloped inclines, while maintaining a steady rhythm. Circling around a tree or bush, while maintaining the same distance from the object, teaches correct maintenance of bend, shape and rhythm. Riding in a steady pace past fearful objects, while implementing leg yields, develops obedience, concentration and rhythm. The horse's freshness on the trail strengthens trot lengthening development. Trotting in shallow water enhances passage and piaffe development. The horse will naturally want to lift his feet. *(Photo 69)* Slight downhill work encourages the horse to sit more on the haunches. Heading towards home, when the horse often desires to jig, can also be used to improve these movements. *(Photo 70)*

Cavalletti work is also a big asset in developing the expression, balance, and regularity. Trot poles properly spaced regarding distance and height are useful in improving collection and extension. Refer to *Cavalletti*, by Reiner Klimke, to obtain more precise information on their implementation in your training program.

Longitudinal exercises, such as expanding and condensing the trot, and transitions between the gaits have a valuable effect on increasing balance, coordination and elasticity of the trot. Lengthening two or three times down the long side or repeatedly on a twenty-meter circle magnifies both the upward and downward transitions. This shorter period of lengthen teaches the horse and rider the feel of the increased power from behind. The downward transition is ridden before the power and balance of the lengthen diminish. Care must be taken to ride the downward transition while maintaining the impulsion created by the upward transition. A good downward is characterized by compression and expression, which maintains the power and balance, while returning to the previous working or collected trot. Robert Dover advises riding the collection in the extension and the extension in the collection. This valuable principle applies to transitions between the gaits as well.

Lateral exercises have a great effect on improving the quality of the trot. They offer increased obedience, suppleness, bending, cadence and engagement. Leg yielding is the most helpful beginning lateral exercise. It can be used along the wall, down

Photo 69 — *Majic and Barbi working piaffe at the beach.*

Photo 70 — *Susanna practicing piaffe on a slope.*

the long side, and on circles. Interspersed with straight work, it's a valuable loosening exercise.

Developing the Canter

The canter is a three beat gait, which can be performed on either the left or right lead. For the right lead, the left hind initiates the stride, followed by the diagonal pair of the left fore and right hind, the right fore, and then a moment of suspension in which all four legs are off the ground. This sequence is reversed for the left lead. The three beat rhythm should maintain an even tempo and display lightness, regularity, engagement and cadence. The quality of straightness should be maintained on both straight and curved lines. The five types of canter as defined by the *USA Equestrian Rule Book* are working, collected, medium, extended, and counter-canter. Refer to the *USA Equestrian Rule Book* for definitions.

Some horses are innately gifted with a correct, balanced, cadenced, air-borne canter with the conformation to support it. If your horse lacks this natural ability, dressage offers an effective means over time to improve his canter. By practicing the various exercises and patterns, the horse's canter will improve in strength, coordination, and quality.

The rider must refrain from bouncing in the saddle in order to improve the canter under saddle. The previously explained lunge exercise of placing the reins in the outside hand while using the inside hand at the pommel to pull the seat more deeply into the saddle can also be used while cantering off the lunge.

In contrast to the walk, the rider's hands and hips follow the movement of the gait in unison. The hands and hips move slightly forward when the horse's neck moves forward and slightly back when the neck comes back. If this following fails to occur, the horse tends to drop behind the vertical, lose balance, suspension and quality of the gait. The degree of following lessens as the collection increases. The rider's legs close quietly when the horse's front end lifts, encouraging the hindquarters to take a more generous step.

The concept of rhythm is equally important to the canter as it is to the trot. Often a horse's unsteady rhythm stems from imbalance. Use of the lunge enables the horse to improve his balance without the added weight of the rider. Refer to *Chapter 8 Lungeing The Horse.* The exercises recommended for improving rhythm in the trot such as counting, carrying a metronome, riding with a partner and riding to music can also improve the canter.

A horse may be rhythmic and yet lack the clear 1, 2, 3 footfall of the canter. The canter can go lateral with the two right legs and two left legs moving almost simultaneously, creating a two beat rhythm. It may also take on a four beat rhythm, losing suspension. This is a result of the horse's splitting the diagonal pair of legs in the canter sequence. Before selecting the appropriate remedy for a two or four beat canter, the rider must determine whether the problem stems from the horse or rider. In terms of the horse, these problems may be the result of poor conformation, imbalance, stiffness, an injury, or weakness. The rider can create these problems by using a bouncing seat or restrictive hands, or failing to adequately drive the horse from behind in the correct timing. In either case, a trainer can assess and help remedy the difficulty.

Initially, many riders have difficulty establishing the correct lead on one side or the other. Timing and preparation play a major role in setting the horse up to take the correct lead. Prior to asking for the canter, the horse must be properly prepared in terms of suppleness, straightness, rhythm and balance. If any of these qualities are absent, repair the deficit before proceeding on to the canter depart.

Whether the strike off to canter occurs from the walk or trot, the aids must be given when the inside fore is on the ground. Count by saying "now" each time the inside fore strikes the ground as you prepare for the upcoming transition. The aids for the depart should be given as you say "now." This specific timing facilitates the strike off on the correct lead.

For best results, the strike off from trot is best obtained from sitting trot. At times, for a green horse or rider, it is more successful to take the canter from rising trot to minimize hollowing and rushing. In this case, it is usually easier to change the posting diagonal to the inside, so that the rider is down in the saddle with the inside fore. This facilitates giving the correct canter depart aids. Additionally, asking for the canter depart on a circle shape or corner supports ease of the transition for a green horse or rider.

Cantering on the trail yields many benefits for developing this gait. The change of scenery often refreshes your horse's attitude. However, some horses may be more nervous on the trail. In this case, practice cantering in circles, around bushes, or on a slight grade to increase the horse's focus on the work. Dealing with the changes in the footing and slope can increase the horse's attention, balance, confidence, and obedience. *(Photo 71)*

Transitions, both to and from the canter, lengthening and shortening within the canter, as well as directional changes in the canter provide essential assistance in improving this gait. They provide fundamental work in training the horse's mind and body. A correct transition demonstrates harmony, suppleness, smoothness, balance, rhythm, confidence and energy. To facilitate achieving these results, the rider must perform each transition while maintaining a correct position, effective use of the aids, and suppleness throughout their application. Through the use of effective transitions, harmonious results of on-the-bitness, overall quality and connection in the canter are enhanced.

Once you have achieved a measure of balance within the canter, you can improve the canter through repeated use of trot-canter transitions. Initially you can focus on circle shapes and later transfer the desired quality onto straight lines. Eventually, transitions can be introduced from walk to canter and canter to walk, as well as to and from the halt. These have a collecting and balancing effect on the canter. Transitions within the gait by lengthening or shortening the stride can be used to increase the overall expression and quality of the canter. Specifically, this exercise increases the horse's power from behind, enhancing the energy, clarity and suspension of the canter. Transitions in figures and patterns, such as riding smaller circles and serpentines, enhance both collection and engagement.

Loosening work done both in the walk and trot carry over to improve the canter. With a relaxed body, especially the back, the horse can move more generously and with greater fluidity. In turn, the mind relaxes. This creates a positive feedback loop, which enhances the gait. Additionally, taking an occasional exaggerated true or counter flexion augments both suppleness and straightness.

Photo 71 — *Barbi cantering Konstellation on a trail around a tree to improve balance and focus.*

The lack of straightness is a common fault in the canter. Frequently the horse breaks laterally to the inside at the base of the neck and carries the haunches to the inside, forming its body into an "L" shape. As previously discussed, straightness is a vital element to the correct training of the horse. The horse's hips are naturally wider than the shoulders, creating an automatic crookedness. An exercise called positioning, in which the horse's shoulders are slightly positioned inward effectively addresses this problem. To achieve positioning, the rider slightly rotates the upper body inward influencing the horse's inner front and hind legs to line up, thereby attaining straightness.

All of the lateral dressage movements, when correctly performed in the canter can greatly benefit the overall quality of this gait. The application of the lateral exercises can be used in many different ways to remedy specific problems such as crookedness, stiffness, improper bending, or lack of collection or engagement. The utilization of an exercise depends on the rider's ability to assess the horse's evasions or weaknesses and respond immediately and effectively. The overall quality of the canter must always be preserved when using the following exercises.

Shoulder in is a frequently used exercise to enhance suppleness and collection both in the canter and transitions around the canter. Intermittent haunches in, ridden on circles, is valuable for suppling, strengthening, and engagement. It also prepares the horse for the pirouette. Usually, this exercise is not practiced on straight lines, because the horse may use it to avoid straightness. Renvers is better used in the trot than the canter as an aid for straightening, since the horse can misinterpret the application of the renvers aids for those of the flying change. Half pass is an excellent exercise for enhancing lateral flexibility, balance, carriage, and engagement. The counter canter is another valuable exercise for building the quality and versatility of the canter. It may be incorporated in a number of ways, but care must be taken to keep the quality of the canter's jump, the correct body alignment and the proper degree of bend throughout the body. Serpentine work with counter canter strengthens the canter and builds collection. Even leg yielding has a positive effect on improving obedience, quality, and straightness.

> "*We must be aware that whatever we practice, consciously or unconsciously, is what we teach.*"

12

The Wisdom Behind Winning

> *"A horse gallops with his lungs, preseverses with his heart, and wins with his character."*
>
> *– Anonymous*

During dressage competition, the rider and horse as a team, present a picture of their physical, mental, emotional and spiritual development to the outside world. Viewed by the educated eye of the judge, fellow competitors and many spectators, the moment of competition takes place amidst a background of excitement, challenge, and vulnerability. This moment crystallizes all the previous moments of practice and preparation into a one-time chance to produce that "beautiful and harmonious ride." As the horse and rider enter at A, they are asking two main questions; 1. "Can we produce a continuous, harmonious flow of the required movements of this test, with no interruptions or repetitions?" 2. "How effective were our results according to the national and international standards?" In this chapter, we'll explore the physical, mental, emotional and spiritual preparations that will enhance competitive performance.

Physical Preparation

When a rider decides to compete, accurate physical preparation is a must. This entails outer physical appearance, in addition to the necessary physical development and fitness for the required test. In competition, remember that you are striving to present a picture of elegance and harmony to the judge. (*Illustration Y*) In dressage this entails correct dress, which is laid out specifically in the USA Equestrian Rule Book.

Before mounting your horse, look in the mirror and make any necessary corrections prior to entering the ring. Your overall appearance should be simple and elegant. This is not the time for jewelry, heavy makeup or floppy hair. At a recent show, Barbi saw a young girl's lovely turnout spoiled by her hair,

Illustration Y — *Scrutinize details for a picture of elegance.*

which, although netted, hung down her back and at every stride of sitting trot, banged against her back. This took away from the picture of a quiet position, even though she was sitting well.

Your clothing should be clean and fit your body properly. At another show, a competitor rode the Training Level test with her undersized coat unbuttoned. Although the ride was lovely, the judge noted, "untidy appearance." This comment underscored the importance of a neat and well-fitted turnout. Your boots should be newly polished and the soles free of debris. Gloves and spurs should be clean and your whip of proper length and in good condition. Finally, avoid colored undergarments, which can be seen through blouses or breeches.

Your horse's turnout is equally important when preparing for competition. His coat should be clean. His nose, bridle path, ears, and fetlocks should be clipped and the dock of his tail should be clipped or braided neatly. In the winter, a body clip may be necessary. His mane should be properly braided, enhancing an overall neat turnout.

Clean tack, which is in good repair and properly fitted, is a must. Check for a clean bit, spurs, and stirrups. Be sure the pad is free of stains and properly fits the saddle. A conservative color such as black, white or cream adds to a picture of elegance. Be sure to remove any wraps prior to entering the arena and know when you may or may not carry a whip.

Physical fitness is imperative for successful competition. The horse and rider must have achieved the degree of physical fitness required to comfortably perform the selected test. Being in shape for competition means that you and your horse have practiced consistently over time for this event. Unfortunately, this reality is sometimes ignored when a horse is thrown into competition too quickly after a lay off. At one show, a rider competed at second level after a three-month pasture layoff. Her horse was overweight and lacked stamina, for it had been returned to work only two weeks prior to the show. Sadly, it sustained a tendon injury due to its lack of physical preparation. In order to present the horse effectively, this same principle holds true for the rider. A physically fit rider will give clearer aids, which makes the horse's job easier.

Mental Preparation

Entering the appropriate level and picking the test best suited for your horse's present ability is essential to competing successfully. Before venturing out to compete, you and your horse should be able to satisfactorily perform most of the movements of the selected test, earning a score of at least "6." Knowing which movements carry a co-efficient of "2" and being able to perform them well, will help you attain a better score. If your work does not meet this level of expertise, knowing the unexpected pressure that always happens when away at a show, you will likely set yourself up for earning lower marks.

Local schooling shows offer an affordable and easily available opportunity to practice a "dry run" competition. This more relaxed atmosphere gives both horses and riders a chance to see what competing entails. Knowing how much time each phase of competition requires from turn out, to warm up, to entering at A can only be understood by doing. For example, if your horse becomes nervous in the competitive environment, you may need to lunge your horse or take a short trail ride prior to your actual warm up. Learning from these schooling shows can help you adapt your preparation for future recognized competitions.

We cannot over-emphasize the importance of knowing your test well. The following three techniques provide ways to ensure recall of your test; draw it, walk it, and visualize it. In drawing your test, use a piece of paper marked out with letters representing a dressage arena. Draw each movement continuously and sequentially, without lifting your pencil. This exercise allows you to experience the flow of the patterns and transitions. Walking the test permits you to physically encode the spatial layout and directional flow of the patterns. For those riders who find spatial learning challenging, this exercise is very helpful. Set up a space either outdoors or indoors and mark your arena with index cards or stones labeled with the appropriate letters. Then proceed to walk through the patterns as required in the test. Repeat this until you can walk the test without prompts. Thirdly, visualize yourself riding the test on your horse in the arena, exactly as you would perform it, step by step. This allows a more detailed mental preparation of the test. For example, say to yourself "half-halt, prepare the bend for the turn at C, half halt again, straighten with the outside rein before the extension across the diagonal, etc." All three of these techniques foster a different way of over-learning your test. Since stress may reduce your ability to recall the test, over-learning compensates for this potential loss.

A reader provides another mental aid for preventing the possibility of riding off course. When a green horse becomes distracted or disobedient, it's easy to momentarily forget what movement comes next. We recommend that you use a reader, when permitted, until you and your horse become more familiar with competition. However, a reader is not a substitute for memorizing your test, since sometimes wind, background noise, or other unexpected problems make hearing your reader's directives difficult.

Another approach to knowing your test is to conceptualize it as a series of individual movements, each with an individual score. Each movement is connected to the whole and the success of each depends on how well it is prepared in advance. However, if one movement has a mistake or problem, you must be able to regroup immediately and continue with full clarity and commitment to what comes next. This was exemplified at a recent ice-skating competition, when Michelle Kwan surprisingly took a fall on the ice. She was up and skating, with a big smile, before the viewer could hardly comprehend what had happened. In fact, the commentator said what an unusual occurrence it was for her to have a problem, but given how well she handled the fall, it seemed that it never even happened. His prediction was true that her scores would probably not even reflect the problem, as the entire rest of her performance was brilliant, bold, and technically very challenging. Her scores were all between 5.8 and 5.9, almost perfect scores. Michelle obviously was conditioned to perform each movement of her routine as an independent piece, not letting one mistake destroy the rest of a beautiful performance.

The same holds true for competing during a dressage test. If a problem arises with your horse on one movement, you must respond quickly. When correcting your horse, be confident and clear so your horse can relax and obey. Because there are two of you out there, it is even more critical that you do this, as your horse will instantly pick up on any tension. His predicted response will be additional tension. Remember that a successful, beautiful performance depends on harmony and grace. Therefore, the outcome is up to you, the rider.

Emotional Preparation

Competition and pressure go hand in hand. To a successful competitor, pressure can increase focus and performance. In this case, pressure is a welcome bonus. However, for many riders, pressure can result in performance anxiety, which can be accompanied by a variety of unpleasant symptoms, such as racing heart beat, sweaty hands, dry mouth, upset stomach, diarrhea, dizziness, headache, and lack of mental clarity. Performance anxiety may range from mild to severe. One of Barbi's students suffered such severe anxiety that she was unable to sleep two days prior to a show. On the day of the competition she was physically exhausted, but her mind was still racing with many fears regarding her ride. Invariably, prior to entering the arena, she had several bouts of diarrhea. Obviously, this level of performance anxiety greatly impeded her ability to show successfully.

Joseph Wolpe, the founder of systematic desensitization, discovered that two opposing responses are incompatible. One response inhibits the other. It is difficult to feel afraid and relaxed at the same time. Wolpe's research determined that individuals, who relaxed while thinking about a feared object, person, or situation, could conquer their fears.

Janet helps riders overcome performance anxiety through systematic desensitization. First, she has the rider picture being in the show arena and focus on tension and anxiety for ten seconds. With this picture in mind, the rider rates the level of anxiety on a scale from 0 (no anxiety) to 10 (severe anxiety). Then the rider pictures a relaxing scene. This could be the beach, a stream by the woods, or a favorite room. While seeing the relaxing scene for about ten seconds, the rider breathes deeply and slowly, and lets go of muscle tension. Envisioning the show arena and then the relaxing scene makes up one set. Most riders report feeling much more relaxed after about fifteen to twenty sets of this process. Often riders experience anxiety reduction of five to seven points.

Riders can practice systematic desensitization daily, one week prior to the show, and then at the show grounds to enhance its effectiveness. Wolpe's method can help reduce the level of performance anxiety from a level of hindrance (any score over a 4) to a level of helpfulness (a score under 4). A low level of anxiety creates an optimal level of alertness and readiness that can enhance performance, but high levels of anxiety reduce performance.

At times, a more depth oriented psychotherapeutic approach may be needed in order to overcome performance anxiety. If systematic desensitization fails to lessen a rider's anxiety, Janet often uses Eye Movement Desensitization and Reprocessing (EMDR), a psychotherapeutic approach designed to reveal and change underlying emotional blocks and/or distorted beliefs that maintain the rider's anxiety. For example, Sarah needed to deal with her belief that she was worthless unless she could win. Since she was riding to prove her self worth, the concept of winning became distorted as the proof of her worthiness as a human being, instead of her level of competence as a rider. Although Sarah knew that this belief was irrational, she felt that it was emotionally true. Helping Sarah separate her performance from her sense of self worth involved about fifteen sessions of therapy. Once she believed that she was a worthy individual regardless of her performance in a horse show, she was able to perform optimally at shows.

Systematic Desensitization and EMDR are two of the most well researched, proven therapeutic treatments for performance anxiety. Other approaches may also be helpful. A trained Psychologist, Marriage and Family Therapist or Licensed Social Worker can help you decide which approach would be most helpful for you. The time, effort, and cost of therapy are often worth the results, not only in the show ring, but also for a rider's emotional growth.

Usually, horses do not welcome pressure, excitement and novelty. In *The Horses Mind*, Lucy Rees explains that horses are defenseless prey rather than predators. Therefore they usually react to new stimuli as if it is dangerous, until proven otherwise. When taken from their familiar home environment, they are bombarded by many novel stimuli, which activate their instinctual "fear program." Fear results in the release of adrenaline, which speeds up the heart rate and increases blood flow to the muscles, preparing the horse to escape. In this moment, the horse filters out everything other than its fear. Many riders forget this important fact, expecting their horse to behave as usual in a strange setting. With this in mind, you can plan a habituation program to help your horse cope with fear prior to competing.

Habituation, the ability to stop responding to a repeated stimuli, is fundamental to the horse's learning process. Although simple, it is the most pervasive learning process in nature. Initially a new stimulus, such as a flower arrangement by the judge's stand, captures the horse's attention and he reacts with fear. However, when exposed repeatedly to the flower arrangement without a harmful consequence, he learns that it is unimportant. At first, his learning is temporary. After a rest period in which the horse is taken away from the feared stimulus, he usually forgets that the flower arrangement poses no threat. Typically in the process of habituation, he reacts less fearfully and habituates more rapidly with each repeated lesson. Repeated short exposures are more effective than a single long exposure.

In addition, habituation must be carried out in a variety of different settings, since habituation may not carry over to other settings. Janet observed this phenomenon in her young five-year-old horse, Degas. Repeated habituation helped Degas walk calmly by the garbage cans in her driveway. However, when a garbage can appeared on the trail, he reverted to his old fear and shied quickly away from it. The habituation had to be repeated again in the new context of the trail.

When helping your horse habituate to new or fearful stimuli, apply combining supportive aids such as half halts, leg yielding, and suppling to provide a familiar anchor. These familiar aids allow your horse to let go of his fear and focus on his work. Let's look at a very common problem of getting past the judge's stand prior to entering at A. In the 45 seconds that precede the ringing bell, give the horse a chance to the see the judge's stand from both the right and left eyes, as well as head on. Promote his acceptance of passing the stand calmly by supporting the horse with your seat and legs as you soften the horse's jaw with your wrists. Obviously, the specific supportive aids will vary moment-to-moment depending on your horse's reaction.

Barbi's young horse Octango needed even more support than strong leg-yield aids at the beginning of his show career. To enter the perimeter of the show arena Barbi used a person walking in front of him to give him the confidence to walk past the scary judge's stand. This technique used the horse's natural tendency to follow and thus attained the desired results. The point is that you pro-actively keep the horse's attention on the rider's aids in the face of the feared stimulus. The use of pro-active aids greatly helps your horse habituate more rapidly.

Thoughtful pre-planning of your training program is necessary to prepare a timid or combative horse for the expected challenges that accompany competing. Octango was talented, with good gaits, size and conformation, but lacked boldness and confidence. When he saw unusual objects, he would become frightened, often backing with strong intention as if to say, "this could be dangerous!" Barbi frequently had to back him where she wanted to go, so he wouldn't have to walk forward into the scary environment. Knowing he needed to build confidence, she exposed him to many new situations, often with another horse or person to guide him by leading the way. Because he had been raised on flat, grassy fields, he was very insecure about contacting bushes, uneven ground, and unexpected objects that are a natural part of trail riding. Over time however, he gained confidence and emotional maturity and began to lead the way in uncertain situations. It was

Photo 72 — *Barbi with a confident and bold Octango.*

wonderful to see his assuredness develop. A horse that previously had to walk backward from here to there could now extend his canter down the long side of an unfamiliar arena with boldness and power. *(Photo 72 on page 99)*

Months prior to an important event for a novice or flappable horse, it is wise to expose the horse to many different locations where he will be expected to work. He should be trailered enough times that such travel is not a major stressor. He should be exposed to his normal work in the new locations so this familiar association can soothe him. Barbi has repeatedly seen that her horse is relieved when he performs familiar dressage work in the setting of the dressage arena, despite the new location. In fact, more frequently than not a smooth performance followed a ragged warm-up, once they entered the familiar competition arena. Prior to competition season, trailering a green horse to new locations, even for trail riding, can help the horse believe that unfamiliar places can be interesting and safe.

When planning departure to a scheduled competition, be sure to arrive at the best time for each horse to acclimate to the change. Some horses need only a couple of hours, but some may need at least a full day. Use the time wisely to walk the horse around the grounds, lunge if necessary and school in several areas in order to calm and habituate him to the new environment. Allow ample time for a relaxed warm-up prior to the time of the class. Too often competitors arrive minutes before their scheduled time, throw their tack on an inadequately groomed horse, and enter at A, without even riding the horse around the outside of the arena. To make matters worse, the rider acts disgusted with the horse after a tense or disobedient ride. Such predictably poor outcomes can be wisely prevented through better planning and preparation.

Arranging a hierarchy of the least to the most difficult situations will help your horse respond more favorably to each new task. It's best to introduce your horse to the least challenging situations first and gradually increase the level of difficulty. The following hierarchy is an example of what your ladder to success might look like.

1. Ride at different times of the day.
2. Ride more than one time per day.
3. Ride in different weather conditions such as wind and rain.
4. Ride with other horses in the arena.
5. Ride under lights.
6. Ride with an audience.
7. Trailer to different locations and ride.
8. Enter local schooling shows.
9. Trailer to large shows and school your horse rather than enter the competition.
10. When entering the show, trailer you horse at least one day prior to the competition and expose your horse to each arena that you will be riding in.

If your horse has difficulty attaining any one goal in your hierarchy, this goal may be broken down into a series of progressive steps. For example in step four, if your horse has difficulty riding with other

Photo 73 — *Deborah and Matt demonstrate positioning a more reactive horse slightly behind and not too close to the lead horse.*

horses in the arena, ride with one calm horse first moving at a safe distance, but slightly behind in the same direction. (*Photo 73, page 100*) Progressively add more horses with changes of direction. Riding in quadrille is excellent for solving this problem.

Maintaining a positive attitude by learning to cope with disappointment is essential for successful competition. Given all the variables that can go wrong in your five to ten minute ride, you will face disappointment at some point during competition. Barbi recalls a highly disappointing experience when she was performing a Grand Prix Pas de Deux with Hilda Gurney at the California Championship Annual Show. They hoped to retire the Western Airlines Perpetual Trophy by winning the class for their third consecutive year. When an enthusiastic crowd clapped in time to their music, Moon Shadow panicked and froze her body next to Hilda's horse, making the execution of the choreography impossible. Needless to say, both riders were extremely disappointed. This example illustrates that some things are beyond a rider's control. When luck doesn't favor you, making the best of the situation empowers you to do your best and maintain a positive attitude. In the above example, Barbi was able to acknowledge that her mare was emotionally unstable and unpredictable. The crowds triggered Moon Shadow's traumatic memories of racing days, when she had frozen in the starting gates. After this experience, Barbi chose less threatening competitions for this particular mare.

Whether your disappointment is as extreme and unusual as this example or simply a lower test score than you had hoped for, learning to cope positively with disappointment is vital. The first step in coping with disappointment is to acknowledge your feelings of anger, hurt, or embarrassment. Verbalizing these feelings to yourself or your coach can help you release the emotional charge.

One of the biggest pitfalls to overcoming disappointment is the "inner critic." This aspect of our personality, usually derived from disapproving parents or other authority figures, re-directs the disappointment over performance to criticism of the self. Watch out for self talk like this. "I'm just a loser." "What a wimp!" "What's wrong with me." These statements usually intensify feelings of helplessness, hopelessness and despair. If you hear your inner voice directing criticism at your personality rather than your performance, stop. Tell your inner critic that performance disappointments do not signal open hunting season on you. Then redirect your attention to your performance.

One of Barbi's students, Katy, felt discouraged after she failed to get the canter on her first attempt to ride a Training Level test. At first she needed to vent her frustration and disappointment, but then she was able to create a more positive attitude by looking at the good points of her ride. Her list looked like this:

1. I rode my very first Training Level test.
2. I got the right leads in my warm-up.
3. My trot and walk work were smooth.
4. My shapes were well executed.

Once a more positive and complete picture is constructed, you are ready to learn from your mistakes. Discussing your mistakes with your coach and observing a video of your ride can help you clarify a better plan of action for the next time. For example, Barbi told Katy that she had warmed up too long, failed to take into account the hot weather, and had not asked clearly for the true canter. These corrections all focus on Katy's actions, which she can improve, not her personality. Katy admitted that during her ride, she had focused on her fear of not getting the correct lead, rather than concentrating on giving correct aids. Prior to her next test, she created a plan to rectify these problems. By using the previous tools to cope with her disappointment, Katy produced successful results on her second ride. As Lanny Bassham, an Olympic and World Champion Rifle Shooter, points out in his book, *With Winning in Mind*, "Your present is not your potential." By focusing on our potential, we can let go of disappointments and move on to positive goals.

Spiritual Preparation

As explained in *Chapter 3: Dressage as Holistic Development*, love and discipline form the basis for spiritual growth. When competition is performed with this attitude, it provides an arena for spiritual enrichment. For Barbi, love is a prime motivation for competition. She loves testing the rapport and understanding of the communication between herself and her horse against the background of the excitement and challenge of competition.

The following story illustrates the sense of spiritual connectedness that Barbi and Celebrate shared at her first Olympic selection trial in 1996, following Celebrate's intermittent six-year lay off.

> *Prior to the vet inspection, I was very anxious because Celebrate was stepping short with his right hind, after a long trailer haul. When my groom trotted him out, I could see that he was not traveling level. At that moment, my chest filled with panic. I feared that after months of preparation for the selection trials, we might not get to compete. My heart went out to him, conveying my deep wish that we could complete our goal together. I visualized Celebrate trotting perfectly before the judges. I knew that he also wanted to succeed in this challenge. I immediately began some massage and stretching techniques and kept him walking, while waiting for my number to be called. However, his unevenness persisted. Finally, our number was called and we began our walk down the aisle in front of the panel of judges. It seemed like an eternity, as I listened to the rhythm of his footsteps. To my amazement, Celebrate sounded perfect. I heard the loudspeaker announce this miraculous occurrence: "Celebrate has passed." I knew that he had extended himself, surpassing his physical limitation, out of his love for me. Tears of joy and gratitude filled my eyes. The next day, we completed our first Grand Prix test in years. It was a clean, exhilarating ride and earned a score of over 60% from the panel of Olympic judges.*

At the selection trials, Barbi clearly experienced the spiritual gift of love, when she and Celebrate competed in oneness and harmony. These peak experiences make competition highly rewarding.

The competitive challenge also offers spiritual growth in the valuable area of discipline, which involves delaying gratification, accepting responsibility, facing the truth, and maintaining balance. One of Barbi's students, Susanna learned the importance of being able to delay gratification, as she began her competitive career with Hallelujah, her new Thoroughbred. As a Second Level rider, she was anxious to enter her horse at First Level. Due to some trauma as a racehorse, Hallelujah was overly reactive to any leg aid. Barbi realized that it would take much disciplined training for this horse to complete the most basic test with confidence. She recommended that Susanna enter him at Training Level in a local schooling show. At first, Susanna was very disappointed. However, after realistically assessing the situation, she was able to select more realistic goals. Together, Barbi and Susanna formulated a training and competitive program that would incorporate competing at First Level the following year. Susanna was able to lower her expectations and concentrate on riding a harmonious Training Level test. She scored over 60% by a recognized judge on their first time out.

The opportunity to grow in the area of accepting responsibility comes with every show. It's so easy to place blame elsewhere, rather than own your part when things don't go as you had hoped. Barbi recalls a recent example of one of her student's growth in accepting responsibility. Robin typically was disorganized in her approach to competing. When she entered the championship show, she had miscounted her qualifying record. Out of five scores, she had three different judges, rather than the required four. This led to her being rejected from the championship show. However, she was able to compete in another section of the show. In warming up for her class, she realized at the last moment that she was preparing for the wrong test. After a disappointing ride, she became angry at her horse. Later, in processing this experience with Barbi, she realized that her lack of organization had created emotional and physical tension, which hampered her performance. This insight addressed her long-term issues of disorganization and blaming, which could be rectified only by accepting responsibility and changing her behavior.

Another important aspect of discipline is the ability to face the truth, however unpleasant it may be. Over a five-year period, Barbi trained Magic, a barely started Holsteiner, to Grand Prix. His body mass and colder temperament stressed Barbi's small frame. She was tempted to continue with Majic so she could compete at the Grand Prix level. Magic showed great promise in his piaffe and passage and liked the challenge of the upper level work. Although difficult, Barbi decided to sell Magic, which allowed her body to heal. The truth is that we all must face limitations at some time in our lives.

Competition can teach us to take things in stride without over reacting or under reacting. Both winning and losing challenge our abilities to remain centered. One might imagine that a famous international rider such as Dr. Reiner Klimke would be egotistical or self-centered. Yet in reality, Dr. Klimke was the opposite. In July of 1999, when Barbi met Dr. Klimke in Germany, his altruistic nature was evident. He spoke not of his accomplishments, but of his pride in his children, his love of his horse, Biotop, and the sport of dressage. Amid his international fame, Dr. Kilmke exhibited the ability to remain in balance.

380
R

13

Reflections on Life Lessons

"*The one moon shows in every pool; in every pool, the one moon.*"

– *Zen Forest Saying*

Since 1970, Barbi has trained countless horses and riders. Teaching dressage has helped her witness the holistic development of both equine and human students. We asked several of Barbi's students to contribute their personal stories about the role of dressage in their journey of personal development. Although most writers focused on either the physical, mental, emotional or spiritual aspect of their growth, several stories incorporated all four aspects. Many were poignant. All were uplifting. We found much inspiration in these stories and hope that you will also.

Carol, one of Barbi's students, recognized the holistic nature of dressage.

> *I have learned to look at the horse as a dancer, some more talented than others, many with varying degrees of training, but all of them capable of wonderful dance. Their very spirit is expressed when they move. I have learned through dressage to connect my spirit with my horse and dance. First, my mind needed focus to connect with my body. Second, my body learned to balance and translate what my mind comprehended. Last, I learned to relax and trust the spirit-to-spirit connection, to be part of the dance.*

Barbi saw tremendous growth in Carol through dressage. When she first began riding, Carol often commented that she felt disconnected from her body. She tended to underestimate her ability and needed a lot of encouragement to move forward into challenges. Yet, her desire to fully feel and express herself with her equine partner fueled her determination to grow. Carol's story reflects the desire to extend beyond our limitations as humans and to join with something greater than ourselves. In doing this, we enhance our own development.

Chuck describes the challenge of learning to ride dressage as a fifty year-old novice.

> *Wisely, Barbi teamed me with the only horse at Sea Horse Ranch that could safely carry my unsteady shifting weight. LittleFoot was a two thousand pound, eighteen hand, gentle Shire. Many of the early lessons were incredibly difficult work, especially when I failed to maintain the forward energy without the aid of Barbi's lunge whip. Until I learned to use the inside of my calves, LittleFoot would simply quit. At times, I felt as if I were trying to empty a concrete truck with each squeeze of my calves. Barbi would ask for more, but I had no more.*

At least I had the good sense to go slowly and to listen carefully to her instructions. I didn't canter for three years. As an artist, I know that truly fine art is more feeling than concept. Finding the feel of a correct aid ultimately worked better for me than learning a series of rote steps. It took time and patience. I learned that my heart and head needed to center on the task at hand, in order to connect with my partner. In turn, I learned to more finely tune my physical and mental balance. I learned to economize energy with proper timing and with coordinated correct aids. And I learned the joy of dressage.

LittleFoot and I rode in our first schooling show after three years of learning to understand and to trust each other. When we trotted into the arena that day, everyone at Sea Horse Ranch gathered at the edge to watch our initiation into the world of competitive dressage. Although we were rewarded with an impressive score, the judge's comment will remain in my memory for a long, long time: "Very quiet and confident, a happy pair."

Chuck's story shows his recognition of his shortcomings, his commitment to obtain expert instruction, and his patience to diligently work towards long-range goals. These qualities helped Chuck attain a sense of competence and joy in his riding. He also transferred this growth to his artwork by learning a new technique involving computer-generated images. Like dressage, creating art on the computer involves much patience and diligence.

The wisdom of patiently following a step-by-step program helped Lauren, a thirteen-year-old, accomplish lessons on her horse, Shy Spirit, that she never dreamed possible. Barbi recalls when Shy Spirit first arrived at Sea Horse Ranch. All three gaits lacked purity, clarity, and regularity. It was impossible for the horse to transition from one gait to another without tripping or shuffling. "This is going to be an interesting project!" Barbi exclaimed.

Lauren worked hard for two years practicing the most simple exercises over and over to teach Shy Spirit to balance over his legs. Just recently, at her first recognized dressage show, Lauren earned a 64% at Training Level, including a "9" on a trot to canter transition. Good dressage, over time, created these astonishing results.

Bonnie's comments stress the importance of fine tuning physical skills in order to communicate more effectively with her horse.

Communicating, giving a specific command, and feeling the response, has shown me that my horse can be taught to be a thinking, responsive, intelligent animal, not just a reactive creature. I realize that riding in balance while effectively using my hands, legs, and seat, influences so much. This has made me aware that I can have an effect not only on the immediate response of the horse, but also on his overall athletic ability.

When we develop athletically as a team, benefits often extend beyond physical performance. Bonnie and her horse, Wraffels, illustrate the connection between physical and emotional growth.

Dressage turned a 14-year-old lawn ornament (he was practically that stiff!) into a supple, balanced, athletic horse. It gave Wraffles the confidence he needed to overcome the fear and tension he felt on the trail. No longer constantly pulling on the bit and jigging if he was last, he now comfortably and reliably can lead or follow with experienced or inexperienced riders. He is no longer a frantic, crooked horse who couldn't even canter in a straight line down the trail, but a safe, trusted mount that has learned to use his mind and body.

Bonnie also shared how working with Wraffles

contributed to her own emotional growth:

> *My self-esteem and confidence have also greatly benefited. As a working mother of three, on many days I must pull from the extraordinary strength that dressage has given me. I am woman, I am invincible, I am a dressage rider!*

In contrast to Bonnie, Cara's story reveals her physical vulnerability and willingness to trust herself to her horse and dressage in order to heal. She avidly pursued dressage, until she suffered a disabling accident, which left her neurologically impaired. To hasten her healing, she turned to dressage and her horse, Jano.

> *Faced with a long recovery in rehabilitation, I found that the patient, methodical approach I had developed for dressage had already given me a head start. I was familiar with taking what I had this instant and making it better in the next, regardless of what I had yesterday. Dressage repaired my body in a way that I would never have believed, until I needed it so much. My neurological impairment left me feeling very disconnected from my body. Some of me didn't work, wasn't there, like the holes in Swiss cheese. Some of me was there, but functioned so poorly that my mind turned off awareness: Swiss cheese gone bad! To feel my horse walking beneath me was healing. The motion seemed to gently shake everything closer to alignment, closer to alive. Riding breathed my life back into me. As my body went back into place, so did my emotions. Whatever the rest of the day drained out, riding put back in. It gave me a better me to take home to the people I love. My horse was not like the physical therapist, who was a necessary part of the day's agenda. He was time out from that agenda. He never looked at me critically to determine how to move each muscle to achieve the maximum benefit. Then and now, he looks at me, sees my heart and heals me spiritually. My horse, my partner, my best friend reminds me that I haven't finished growing yet.*

Cara's story emphasizes the gradual, systematic physical development that becomes especially important when dealing with physical challenges. When we witness stories that tell of such dramatic progress from dressage's systematic approach, like Cara we experience the awe of the gift of dressage. For Cara, dressage not only restored her physically and emotionally, but also spiritually.

Dressage helps us develop mentally. Our mental habits, frequently manifest physically. Wendy shows how mental blocks can be overcome through riding.

> *By nature, I am a very organized person and I don't deviate easily from established habits. One of the hardest things for me to learn in dressage has been flexibility. I have to work very hard to keep my arms from becoming stiff and unyielding. Dressage has been instrumental in teaching me to relax and go with the flow. I have learned that it is possible to stay in control, while maintaining the flexibility to deal with all the unexpected situations that are a part of life.*

Wanda, a physician, acknowledged that she is a very exacting perfectionist. Through dressage, she has grown in self-forgiveness. In telling her story, she listed several new and more positive cognitions that she learned through riding.

> 1. *I can appreciate small improvements.*
> 2. *I can enjoy my horse.*
> 3. *It's okay to ask for help. I don't have to know everything.*
>
> *These new beliefs, learned through dressage, have contributed to my greater enjoyment and appreciation of life. In this new awareness I remind myself "Don't grip and strangle my life. Lighten, lighten, lighten!"*

Barbi has witnessed much growth in young children through dressage. Although this growth tends to be holistic, she noted the dramatic mental change in one of her six-year-old students. When Karolyn began lessons, she was unable to conceptualize and verbalize what she learned in her lesson. Through repeated practice, she gradually was able to understand and state various concepts about riding. At the end of her lesson, when Barbi asked what she had learned that day, she stated clearly, "I must sit up and give a clear aid. I must give the aid clearly until Sara understands the aid, then reward."

Karolyn's parents expressed their delight in her growth, saying, "We've seen her verbal skills, critical thinking, and decision making improve dramatically. We didn't anticipate how much life learning would occur in her learning to ride, and we are very pleased with the results." They've noticed a big change in their child's behavior at school. Last year in first grade, Karolyn never responded verbally when her teacher asked her for feedback. She looked down or began to cry. This year in second grade, Karolyn responds easily to questions and reads aloud to the class. Karolyn even remarked, "I'm not shy anymore!"

Many of the stories we received talked about how riders cleared emotional blocks through their dressage riding. As you can guess, the most common emotional block was fear, human fear and equine fear, resulting in a fight or flight response. As riders, this either leads to fighting with our horse or retreating in panic. Kathy first confronted her fear through her dressage training.

> *My most important dressage lesson has been to deal with fear. I know it sounds odd to be talking about dressage lessons, where one should be learning about shoulder-ins or contact, instead of coping with fear. But through my lessons, I've learned to control my fear, to keep from transmitting it to my sensitive mare. I've always done panic really well. Not that anyone would have ever known, because I've managed to hide it under the guise of busy efficiency. This no longer worked for me from my new perspective of five feet above the ground. Jesse, the great equalizer, saw right through my facade and held me accountable for my fear. This was the first time anyone had ever called me on it. Of course, my realization of this didn't help the fear. It actually made it worse, as I worried more about how she was going to react to my serious case of nerves. She reacted more violently and then I would follow suit. It became a vicious circle.*
>
> *Barbi encouraged me to accept the fact that Jesse is hot and may try to buck. That's just something that she does. From now on that will be the starting point. Barbi coached, "Deal with it with as little fuss as you need and move on from there. Change your attitude and it will change your mare's attitude." Barbi saw through my fear and helped me see that I was creating almost every situation myself. My mare wasn't viciously trying to unseat me. She was just very tuned into my feelings.*
>
> *Well, needless to say, learning to deal with fear has affected all aspects of my life. I still feel fear, I'm just able to deal with it more constructively now. I don't get so wrapped up in it that it completely consumes me anymore. It's very humbling to know that my "disguise" was so transparent, but so freeing to look at my fear from a different perspective. I now have the key to unlock fear's hold on me.*

With Barbi's help, Kathy learned to face her fear. Dressage also helps our equine partners overcome emotional blocks. When Gretchen first purchased her five Arabians, they all shared a common inability to focus. They noticed everything that did or didn't happen around them. Their bodies were tense, their necks high, and their gaits short. Gretchen recounts how dressage helped her horses grow emotionally:

> *Through dressage, my horses have calmed greatly, and become more attentive horses. In turn, I can connect better with them, making riding very pleasurable for all of us. These horses have been challenged in a variety of disciplines including quadrille, jumping, trail riding in the ocean and mountains. They are now very reliable partners.*

When we first began writing this book, we hesitated on including the spiritual aspect of dressage as development. We wondered that we might be too "out there." However, we felt from our own experience that any book on riding and holistic development would fall short if we failed to consider spirituality. Interestingly enough, we received many stories that focused on this aspect.

Earlier we explored the four tools of discipline, delaying gratification, accepting of responsibility, dedication to truth, and balancing. Gail's story especially shows how accepting responsibility and dedicating oneself to truth contribute to spiritual growth both in dressage as well as life.

> *Dressage strips away the layers of human baggage; fears and excuses. In order to create beauty, harmony, lightness, and straightness, I must become those things. That is the secret. Whatever I want from my equine partner, because I want the purest of what he can give, I must first offer him. One day, my horse, Condor, completely shut down. I was in total denial of my part in it. Out of desperation, I apologized to him. I realized that I needed to relax and focus on giving, rather than taking. When I did that, amazingly, the bounce returned to Condor's stride. The more responsible I became, the more responsive he became. When I ask, "What can I do to make it better," the defensiveness leaves, the harmony comes, and the partnership becomes whole.*

Paula, a local artist, spoke of the benefits of achieving balance through dressage. When she finds this place through her riding, she is able to carry it out into her art as well as the rest of her life.

> *There are not many things in life that bring as great a feeling of joy to me, as being with my horse. As I learn to locate my center of balance, I discover a peaceful, poised, and powerful feeling. In that state of mind, I can easily bring my mare, Illustrate, to that same center and give gentle reminders to keep her there.*

This description is exemplified by Paula's painting, entitled "Celebrate" appearing on the cover of this book. In this picture, the rider extends her arms laterally with no reins and canters joyfully, with her head thrown back and hair blowing in the wind. Once before quadrille practice, Janet, having just admired this painting, asked Paula to demonstrate this joyful balance. Without a word, Paula dropped Illustrate's reins and cantered in perfect balance. Paula commented on this sense of centeredness.

> *It's like in drawing when I'm able to catch the line of a form perfectly. There is a sense of refinement and quality that I strive for in my daily life. When I've found it in my riding, I'm better able to maintain it in the rest of my life.*

As we've seen from these stories, the study and practice of dressage offers valuable wisdom for conducting life. Sharon's insight sum up the holistic benefits of dressage.

> *It is truly hard to distinguish where the lessons of dressage leave off and those of life begin. Growth through dressage encompasses the mind, emotions, body, and spirit. Only through practicing dressage have I begun to feel mentally organized and focused. Clarity and definition have replaced clutter and confusion. An entire new level of concentration,*

communication, and commitment has emerged. Physically, my chest has unfolded and my form now stands tall and proud. My muscles feel liberated and work independently from each other. Inferiority has been replaced by self-esteem, uncertainty with confidence and pessimism with pride. I have enhanced creativity through an untapped dimension. I have discovered the exhilaration a dancer knows, when I hear and feel the music in the simple melody and rhythm of the gaits.

Barbi's love of Celebrate allowed her to defer the gratification of competing and helped her find the dedication and discipline to support his healing over a six-year period. Barbi recalls that Celebrate was a champion from the moment they began their competitive career in 1985.

That year he was named the California Dressage Society (CDS) First Level Horse of the Year and USA Equestrian National First Level Champion. He won some title every year thereafter, as we progressed through the levels to Grand Prix. Then in the summer of 1990, we spent a month in training with Robert Dover at USET headquarters in Gladstone. Celebrate moved solidly into Grand Prix.

Just a few months later, however, Celebrate sustained an injury, while I was out of town teaching a clinic. He developed lymphangitis, a painful swelling of the leg's lymph vessels and nodes. His prognosis was poor. For a month, my horse lived at the veterinary hospital, where he struggled to walk. With limited improvement, he returned home, but was allowed only a short walk in-hand for exercise each day. Soon he became so frustrated and depressed that he began digging 18 inch holes and was aggressive to everyone but me. As a result of his frustration, he developed pedalosteitis, inflammation of the coffin bone in his front feet, then back problems. It was months before he could exercise.

Our ranch is a twenty minute walk from the ocean. My veterinarian agreed that walks in the salt-water could speed Celebrate's healing. The first trips to the beach were painful for both Celebrate and me. At first, he could only walk ten minutes in the water. Over time, his exercise period was extended. Eventually, we added trot work in the water. It was thrilling to see him gain strength and soundness. After about a year and a half, Celebrate was feeling sound in walk and trot. That's when he injured a tendon on his one good leg and required another layoff. I was devastated, but determined to nurse my champion back to health again.

About a year later, we competed in five FEI level competitions: one at Prix St. George, one at Intermediare I, and three at Grand Prix. I was excited to be back in competition. Celebrate was proud. He loves to perform. But shortly before the CDS Annual Show in l994, again when I was away teaching a clinic, he suffered another setback. While cast in his stall, he sustained hard and soft-tissue damage. His chances were one in ten for a full recovery. We embarked on yet another year of rehabilitation. His veterinarian remarked in amazement that Celebrate had sustained and recovered from at least six serious injuries within six years. "It's a miracle," he said, adding, "Anyone of those injuries could have ended a horse's career!"

After seventeen months of rebuilding Celebrate's strength and then beginning a real dressage program, I decided to bring him out for a demonstration of upper-level movements at one of my schooling shows at the ranch. He was braided and wrapped, and I dressed out in my tails. We rode the Prix St. George test and had no more entered the arena and halted at X, when he lit up. The extended trot across the diagonal seemed to take only ten strides. I could hardly keep him from passaging the trot work. He was proud and excited to be riding a test again. I had tears in my eyes. The crowd went crazy. Once again, I realized how much we both love to dance together.

Several months later, we rode again with Robert Dover. He was thrilled with Celebrate's comeback. We set a goal to compete in the upcoming Olympic selection trials. I now had a deadline: four months to pull it all together. In May of 1996 at the Paddock Riding Club in Los Angeles, Celebrate performed beautifully with heart and soul at his first selection trial. As we passaged down centerline, he felt buoyant, powerful and proud. Tears welled in my eyes when we placed our final halt and saluted. Walking out of the arena, my mind filled with memories of the six-year struggle that led to this miracle moment. My heart swelled with pride and admiration for my equine partner.

I feel proud and privileged to own and work with a true champion of dressage. There are few people, let alone horses, who persevere in spite of adversity with such grace and heart. I salute Celebrate and thank him for allowing me to deeply understand the true meaning of the relationship between horse and rider. I have learned much about myself, about the potential between horse and rider, and about the unique greatness of my champion, Celebrate.

Barbi's story illustrates love and discipline. She extended herself remarkably to help Celebrate heal. Although Barbi's story is one of loss as well as gain, her admiration and love for Celebrate outshines the shadow of the ordeal of his healing. This exemplifies true spiritual growth, for out of this extension of the self, the giver receives the gift of an expanded sense of self.

As many of these stories demonstrate, dressage offers developmental lessons for both the horse and rider that extend beyond the arena. Dr. Josef Knipp, a renowned international judge recognized this when he said, "More than any other art, classical riding is connected to the wisdom of living, because so many of its principles are maxims for living as well." He refers to the higher purpose of dressage as having to do with the harmony of two spirits. This in fact, is also the wisdom offered by life. When we are in harmony with the self and the world around us, we sense the higher purpose of living. What Dr. Knipp says of riding that lacks joy, is also true of life that lacks joy. He challenges us to continue asking ourselves: "If this magnificent, generous, sensitive creature doesn't nicker happily when he sees me... What is the point?"

> *Thus, man and horse should try to become a single entity . . . there is nothing more beautiful on earth. If one reaches this only now and then, it has been worth the effort.*
>
> –Walter Zettl

Glossary of Terms

Above the Bit
A head position in which the horse resists the rider's hands by poking his muzzle outward and upward, hollowing his back, and leaving his hocks out behind him.

Acceptance
Lack of evasion, resistance, or protest. The horse willingly allows the maintenance of a steady contact, the application of the aids, and/or the placement of the rider's weight.

Aids
The means by which the rider communicates with his horse by use of the rider's aids. The natural aids are: The legs, seat, back, weight, and hands. The artificial aids are: The whip, spur, and voice.

Activity
Energy, liveliness, often referring to that of the hindlegs.

Against the Bit
The horse presses his mouth against the bit with a rigid or un-yielding neck, poll, or jaw.

Balance
Relative distribution of the weight of horse and rider upon the front and hindlegs (longitudinal balance), and the left and right legs (lateral balance). The horse is in good balance when the weight is distributed evenly left and right, and sufficiently toward the hindlegs that he can manage the task at hand. Loss of balance means the sudden increase of weight onto the fore-hand and/or to one side.

Basics
The basics form the correct foundation for the progressive training of the horse. These are the regularity of the rhythm; suppleness and relaxation; acceptance of the bridle with connection through the body; riding forward with impulsion, and straightness in balance; and finally, the development of collection and carrying power.

Correctness of the basics is indicated by improvement of the quality of the gaits, the physique of the horse, the attitude, and rideability of the horse.

Beat
A footfall within a gait made by a hoof, or pair of hooves striking the ground. The walk has four beats, the trot two beats, and the canter three beats.

Behind the Bit
An evasion in which the horse shrinks back from the bit or contact. The head may or may not be behind the vertical. Accurate visual diagnosis of this condition may not be possible but can be verified by the rider.

Behind the Vertical
The head position in which the silhouette of the horse's face drops behind an imaginary vertical line.

Bend

The laterally arced position in which the horse's body appears to form an even curve from poll to tail. Examples of faulty bend are; bending only in the neck, only at the base of the neck, or bent toward the wrong direction.

Blocked

Impaired in an elastic connection due to sustained muscular contraction.

Cadence

Steady tempo with marked accentuation of the rhythm and beat, with emphasized springiness.

Carriage

The posture of the horse, most easily evaluated when viewing the horse's profile or outline.

Clarity

Marked distinction between the footfalls of a gait.

Collection

The horse's frame between the rider's legs and hands is shortened, the hocks are more engaged under his body, the forehand is elevated, and the neck is more raised and arched. The tempo of the gait remains the same but the horse covers less ground as he lifts his legs higher taking shorter, more expressive, cadenced steps.

Confidence

The boldness and self-assurance with which the horse performs, and the trust in his partnership with his rider.

Connection

State in which there is no blockage, break, or slack in the circuit that joins the horse and rider into a single harmonious unit. The unrestricted flow of energy and influence from the rider to and throughout the horse, and back to the rider.

Contact

Reins stretched such that they form a straight line, not a loop. Correct contact, or acceptance of contact, is determined by the elasticity of the connection between the horse and rider. The horse accepts the rider's hands with a soft, quiet, rounded outline of his top muscling.

Crookedness

Misalignment of the horse's body from poll to tail, lack of directness of direction or alignment to a pattern.

Cross Canter

The horse canters on one lead in front and the other lead behind, also called disunited.

Disobedience

Willful determination to avoid doing what is asked, or determination to do what is not asked.

Elasticity

The ability or tendency to stretch and contract the musculature smoothly, giving the impression of stretchiness or springiness.

Engagement

Increased flexion of the joints of the hindlegs and the lumbosacral joint allowing the horse to bring the hindlegs more under his body for increased balance and weight carriage. As the croup is lowered, there is a relative raising of the forehand.

Expression

Cadence.

Extension

At trot and canter, a pace in which the horse maintaining an uphill balance, shows maximum length of stride through greatest forward thrust and utmost reach.

At walk, a pace which covers as much ground as

possible with each stride, showing greatest push from behind and maximum reach.

Falling In, Falling Out

Lateral deviation of the shoulders or haunches caused by loss of balance or evasion.

Flexibility

The ability to move the joints freely.

Flexion

The horse responds to the rider's legs and hands by bending his joints. Lateral and longitudinal flexion usually refers to the horse yielding in his poll and relaxing his jaw.

Forehand

The horse's head, neck, front legs, shoulders, and withers.

Forward

To or toward the direction that is ahead or in front of the horse, or moving or tending toward that direction.

Freedom

Full range of motion of the front and hind limbs.

Free Walk

A pace of relaxation in which the horse is allowed complete freedom to stretch out and lower his head and neck. Both the strides and frame are lengthened. The reins can be long or loose.

Gait

The horse has three natural gaits – the walk, trot, and canter.

Half-Halt

A momentary increase of collection, or an effect of the aids which increases the attention and improves the balance of the horse, for example to prepare for a change of direction or transition to another gait. It is achieved through driving the horse forward with the seat and legs to a somewhat restraining and suppling hand, followed by a moment of lightness of the hand.

Hollow Back

Sagging or depressed back caused by slackness or tense contraction of the back muscles.

Impulsion

Forward, upward thrust, giving energy and brilliance to the horse's movement.

Inside

The side away from the rail, or on the inside of any curve or circle. The direction toward which the horse should be positioned (laterally) or bent.

Irregular

Impure, unlevel, or uneven. Can be momentary or pervasive, and may or may not be due to unsoundness.

Lateral

1. To the side, as in flexion, bend, suppleness, or direction of travel.

2. Impurity in walk resulting in pace like steps or in canter, both front and hind legs on one side hitting the ground at almost the same moment.

Leg-yield

A lateral movement used to teach obedience and suppling, whereby the horse moves forward and sideways away from the asking leg while staying longitudinally aligned.

Lengthening

Elongation of the stride and the outline of the horse while maintaining the same tempo and balance as in the corresponding working pace.

Lightness

Referring to the self-carriage of the horse being light on its feet and/or light on the reins.

Longitudinal
Referring to the long axis of the horse's body as in back to front or front to back.

Marching
Purposeful steps in the walk.

Medium
At trot and canter, a pace at which the horse shows a length of stride between that of collection and extension, and a more uphill balance, more forward and upward thrust, and more reach than in his working pace. The movement produced is rounder than that of extension.

At walk, a pace with a length of stride between that of the collected and extended walk, showing a clear overstep, good march from behind and good reach.

On the aids
The horse maintains a good connection through his body to all the aids responding instantly and generously without resistance.

On the bit
The horse offers a light, elastic, and quiet acceptance of contact with the rider's hands through the reins. The neck remains stretched with lateral and longitudinal flexion as required. The horse moves forward actively from the hind legs with balance and impulsion in response to the rider's aids with his neck raised or lowered (depending on the degree of collection or extension).

On the forehand
The horse places too much weight on the front legs for the task at hand demonstrating poor longitudinal balance.

Outline
The profile of the horse showing the horse's carriage or posture.

Outside
The side closest to the rail, or outside of any curve or circle. In lateral movements, the direction away from which the horse should be bent.

Overstep
The placement of the hind foot in front of the print of the front foot.

Pace
1. Any of the variations within each gait: collected, working, lengthened, medium, or extended.

2. A gait in which both front and hind legs on each side move almost in unison, not correct for dressage.

Poll
The highest point of the horse's skull, between the ears.

Position
1. The lateral flexion at the horse's poll so that the horse looks slightly to the left or the right.

2. The rider's posture in the saddle.

Purity
Correctness of the order of the footfalls and phases of the gaits.

Regularity
Correctness of the gait, involving purity, evenness, and levelness. Irregularities may be momentary or pervasive, and may or may not be caused by unsoundness.

Relaxation
Calmness, without anxiety, nervousness, or undesired muscular tension.

Resistance
Physical opposition by the horse against the rider, such as getting his tongue over the bit, wringing his tail, hollowing his back, pulling on the reins, throwing the head in the air, etc.

Rhythm
The characteristic sequence of the footfalls within each gait. The walk has a four-beat rhythm, the trot has two-beats and the canter has three-beats. The rhythm should always remain steady and consistent.

Roundness
The convexity of the profile of the horse's topline.

Seat
The rider's balanced posture in the saddle. The position should be erect but relaxed, with the seat in the center and deepest part of the saddle. The body should follow the horse's movements and be able to give effective aids without losing correct alignment.

Self-Carriage
State in which the horse carries itself without taking support or balancing on the rider's hands.

Stiff
Inability to flex the joints or stretch the musculature smoothly and effectively enough for the necessary movement or exercise. Stiffness issues can refer to both horse and rider.

Straight
1. Following a direct line of travel.

2. Alignment of the horse's backbone to the track on which he is traveling. The hind feet should travel directly into the prints of the forefeet.

Stride
Cycle of the horse's leg movements that is completed when they return to their initial position. Length of stride refers to the amount of ground covered by the above sequence.

Submission
The yielding of the horse's will to that of the rider, as revealed by a constant attention, willingness, and confidence in the attitude of the horse, as well as by the harmony and ease with which the horse and rider work together. The movements performed are correctly executed, displaying proper bend, acceptance of the rider's aids, and correct balance.

Suppleness
Ability to smoothly adjust the longitudinal carriage and lateral bend or flexion without losing the flow, elastic movement or balance.

Suspension
The moment in the trot or canter when the horse has all four feet off the ground.

Swinging Back
The alternating contracting and relaxing of the horse's back muscles rhythmically which give spring to the gaits and allow the thrust from the hindlegs to propel the horse forward with elasticity.

Swinging Head
The horse's face moves left and right, often in time with the steps indicating incorrect acceptance of the bit.

Tempo
Rate of repetition of the rhythm of the footfalls or strides.

Tense
Referring to the horse's mental or emotional state as being nervous or anxious. Referring to the horse's physical state as displaying taut, contracted muscles inhibiting fluent movement.

Throughness

The supple, unblocked, connected state of the horse's musculature that allows a fluid flow of energy from back to front and front to back, receiving and transmitting the rider's aids throughout its body smoothly.

Tilting

Carriage of the horse's head tipped so that one ear is carried higher than the other.

Topline

The outline of the horse from the tip of the ears along the top of its neck and back to the tail.

Tracking up

The horse's hind feet step into the tracks of the front feet.

Transition

A change of gait, pace within a gait, or movement. All transitions should be made smoothly and quietly.

Uneven

Unequal in length of steps.

Unlevel

Unequal height of steps or carrying of weight on both sides.

Uphill

1. Referring to the horse's longitudinal balance as in carrying more weight on the hindlegs from lowering the croup.

2. Conformationally the horse's withers being placed higher on the horse's body than the top of the croup.

Working

An energetic and relaxed pace performed by the horse which shows a length of stride between that of collected and medium. That pace for each horse whereby he most effectively carries himself with ease and activity.

References

Alberti, R. and Emmons, M. *Your Perfect Right.* San Luis Obispo, California: Impact Publishers, Inc., 1995.

Alberti, R. and Emmons, M. *Accepting Each Other.* San Luis Obispo, California: Impact Publishers, Inc., 1991.

Bassham, Lanny. *With Winning In Mind.* Wilsonville, Oregon: Book Partners, Inc., 1995.

Blinks, Susan. "The Pyramid of Training." *Dressage & CT.* Feb. 1997: 44-46.

Chopra, Deepak, M.D. *Ageless Body, Timeless Mind.* New York, New York: Harmony Books, 1993.

Cloverleaf Dressage Videotapes (Producer). *The Aachen Composite: A Right Brained Study of the FEI Movements and Tests.* (Videotape). Columbia, CT: Cloverleaf Dressage Videotapes.

Connelly, K. and Whittlesey, M. *Dressage Insights: Excerpts from Experts.* Boonsboro, Maryland: Half Halt Press, Inc., 1994.

Ellis, A. and Harper, R. *A New Guide to Rational Living.* No. Hollywood, California: Wilshire Book Company, 1975.

Gurney, Hilda. "Blueprint for Success." *Dressage Today.* Sept. 1996: 62-69.

Klimke, Reiner. *Basic Training of the Young Horse.* London, England: J.A. Allen & Company Limited, 1985.

Klimke, Reiner. *Cavalletti.* London, England: J.A. Allen & Company Limited, 1969.

Klimke, R. and Werner, E. *Klimke On Dressage.* Middletown, Maryland: Half Halt Press, Inc., 1992.

Kyrklund, Kyra and Lemkow, Jytte. *Dressage with Kyra.* North Pomfret, Vermont: Trafalgar Square Publishing, 1998.

Wynmalen, Henry. *Dressage: A Study of the Finer Points of Riding.* Cranbury, New Jersey: A.S. Barnes & Co. Inc, 1952.

Millman, Dan. *The Inner Athlete: Realizing Your Fullest Potential.* Walpole, New Hampshire: Stillpoint Publishing, 1994.

O'Connor, Sally. *Common Sense Dressage.* Middletown, Maryland: Half Halt Press, 1990.

Peck, Scott, M.D. *The Road Less Traveled.* New York, New York: Simon & Schuster, 1978.

Rees, Lucy. *The Horse's Mind.* New York, New York: Prentice Hall Press, 1985.

Savoie, Jane. *More Cross-Training: Build A Better Performance Horse with Dressage.* North Pomfret, Vermont: Trafalgar Square Publishing, 1998.

Schwartz, B. and Robbins, S., eds. *Psychology of Learning and Behavior.* New York, New York: W.W. Norton & Company, Inc., 1995.

Taylor, P., Weyler, R. and Ingrasci, R., eds. *Chop Wood, Carry Water.* New York, New York: G.P. Putnam's Sons, 1984.

Tellington-Jones, Linda. *Getting in T Touch.* North Pomfret, Vermont: Trafalgar Square Publishing, 1995.

United States Dressage Federation, Inc. *Glossary of Dressage Judging Terms*. Lincoln, Nebraska.

USA Equestrian Rule Book 2003. Lexington, KY: USA Equestrian, Inc., 2003.

Zahn Cheek, Marilyn. "Riding With T'ai Chi." *Dressage Today.* Aug. 1996: 50-54.

Notes

Notes

Notes

Notes

Notes

Notes

Notes

About the Authors

Barbi Breen-Gurley has taught dressage to students of all ages, abilities and riding goals since obtaining her BHSAI from Moat House, England in 1970. Well respected national and international instructors such as Hilda Gurney, Robert Dover, Laurie Doyle, Willy Arts, and Albrecht Heidemann have helped Barbi develop her own riding skills. She has trained several horses to the Grand-Prix level and won numerous, state, regional and national championships. She is a USDF Bronze, Silver & Gold Medallist. She has been long listed or placed on the Developing Rider list numerous times. She is a S rated USAE Dressage Judge.

Janet Emmons obtained her M.A. in English and Educational Specialist degree from the University of Iowa and completed her M.S. in Psychology from California Polytechnic University. In private practice, she has worked with many equestrians, helping them overcome fear, performance anxiety, low self-esteem, anger and other emotional blocks to their riding progress. She has trained with Barbi since 1986. Her experiences as a therapist and rider helped her realize that the challenges we face in riding, such as staying centered, improving our connection, and preparing for transitions have implications for the way we conduct our lives.

About the Illustrator

Paula Zima states that her mission is "to create delightful art for the world to enjoy." She has done this through her illustration, public art, sculpture and paintings. She has been a dressage and horsemanship enthusiast for many years and credits Barbi for teaching her a firm foundation in the art of dressage.